THE TURBULENT 60s

1968

Mary E. Williams, *Book Editor*

Bruce Glassman, *Vice President*
Bonnie Szumski, *Publisher*
Scott Barbour, *Managing Editor*
David M. Haugen, *Series Editor*

GREENHAVEN
PRESS ®

THOMSON

™

GALE

San Diego • Detroit • New York • San Francisco • Cleveland
New Haven, Conn. • Waterville, Maine • London • Munich

© 2004 by Greenhaven Press. Greenhaven Press is an imprint of The Gale Group, Inc., a division of Thomson Learning, Inc.

Greenhaven® and Thomson Learning™ are trademarks used herein under license.

For more information, contact
Greenhaven Press
27500 Drake Rd.
Farmington Hills, MI 48331-3535
Or you can visit our Internet site at http://www.gale.com

ALL RIGHTS RESERVED.
No part of this work covered by the copyright hereon may be reproduced or used in any form or by any means—graphic, electronic, or mechanical, including photocopying, recording, taping, Web distribution or information storage retrieval systems—without the written permission of the publisher.

Every effort has been made to trace the owners of copyrighted material.

Cover credit: © Malcolm Lubliner/CORBIS
Library of Congress, 33, 42, 82
National Archives, 22, 50, 91

LIBRARY OF CONGRESS CATALOGING-IN-PUBLICATION DATA

1968 / Mary E. Williams, book editor.
 p. cm. — (The turbulent 60s)
Includes bibliographical references and index.
ISBN 0-7377-1840-4 (lib. bdg. : alk. paper) —
ISBN 0-7377-1841-2 (pbk. : alk. paper)
 1. United States—History—1961–1969—Sources. 2. A.D. nineteen sixty-eight—Sources. I. Williams, Mary E., 1960– . II. Turbulent 60s.
E846.A186 2004
973.923—dc22   2003057137

Printed in the United States of America

CONTENTS

August 8, Richard M. Nixon appealed to America's "quiet majority," promising to find an honorable way to end the Vietnam War and to reestablish security in America's streets.

FOREWORD

The 1960s were a period of immense change in America. What many view as the complacency of the 1950s gave way to increased radicalism in the 1960s. The newfound activism of America's youth turned an entire generation against the social conventions of their parents. The rebellious spirit that marked young adulthood was no longer a stigma of the outcast but rather a badge of honor among those who wanted to remake the world. And in the 1960s, there was much to rebel against in America. The nation's involvement in Vietnam was one of the catalysts that helped galvanize young people in the early 1960s. Another factor was the day-to-day Cold War paranoia that seemed to be the unwelcome legacy of the last generation. And for black Americans in particular, there was the inertia of the civil rights movement that, despite seminal victories in the 1950s, had not effectively countered the racism still plaguing the country. All of these concerns prompted the young to speak out, to decry the state of the nation that would be their inheritance.

The 1960s, then, may best be remembered for its spirit of confrontation. The student movement questioned American imperialism, militant civil rights activists confronted their elders over the slow progress of change, and the flower children faced the nation's capitalistic greed and conservative ethics and opted to create a counterculture. There was a sense of immediacy to all this activism, and people put their bodies on the line to bring about change. Although there were reactionaries and conservative holdouts, the general feeling was that a united spirit of resistance could stop the inevitability of history. People could shape their own destinies, and together they could make a better world. As sixties chronicler Todd Gitlin writes, "In the Sixties it seemed especially true that History with a capital H had come down to earth, either interfering with life or making it possible: and that within History, or threaded through it, people were living with a supercharged density: lives were bound up with one another, making claims on one another, drawing one another into the common project."

Perhaps not everyone experienced what Gitlin describes, but few would argue that the nation as a whole was left untouched by the radical notions of the times. The women's movement, the civil rights movement, and the antiwar movement left indelible marks. Even the hippie movement left behind a relaxed morality and a more ecological mindset. Popular culture, in turn, reflected these changes: Music became more diverse and experimental, movies adopted more adult themes, and fashion attempted to replicate the spirit of uninhibited youth. It seemed that every facet of American culture was affected by the pervasiveness of revolution in the 1960s, and despite the diversity of rebellions, there remained a sense that all were related to, as Gitlin puts it, "the common project."

Of course, this communal zeitgeist of the 1960s is best attributed to the decade in retrospect. The 1960s were not a singular phenomenon but a progress of individual days, of individual years. Greenhaven Press follows this rubric in The Turbulent Sixties series. Each volume of this series is devoted to the major events that define a specific year of the decade. The events are discussed in carefully chosen articles. Some of these articles are written by historians who have the benefit of hindsight, but most are contemporary accounts that reveal the complexity, confusion, excitement, and turbulence of the times. Each article is prefaced by an introduction that places the event in its historical context. Every anthology is also introduced by an essay that gives shape to the entire year. In addition, the volumes in the series contain time lines, each of which gives an at-a-glance structure to the major events of the topic year. A bibliography of helpful sources is also provided in each anthology to offer avenues for further study. With these tools, readers will better understand the developments in the political arena, the civil rights movement, the counterculture, and other facets of American society in each year. And by following the trends and events that define the individual years, readers will appreciate the revolutionary currents of this tumultuous decade—the turbulent sixties.

The Year of Rage

The year 1968 was one of the most chaotic years in American history. A potent mixture of idealism and frustration, hope and bitterness, diversity and discord mark 1968 as the pivotal year of the decade, the year that would come to symbolize all the contradictions commonly implied in the phrase "the sixties." The year's beginning was punctuated by a disturbing intensification of the Vietnam War and an increasing national disillusionment with the conflict as the nightly news brought images of the war—and reports of rising casualties—into American living rooms. Spring arrived with more shocking news: Two bright young political leaders, civil rights activist Martin Luther King Jr. and presidential hopeful Robert F. Kennedy, were assassinated. Their untimely deaths were especially devastating because these two men had advocated the kind of idealistic social change that a growing number of students and activists were working to bring to fruition. What came to fruition instead in 1968 was rage. Bitter racial tensions erupted into riots, and conflicts among student protesters, antiwar demonstrators, politicians, and police escalated into violent bloodbaths. America in 1968 seemed on the verge of falling apart.

Racial Strife

Racial conflicts and street rage were nothing new to America in 1968. The spring and summer months of several previous years had witnessed numerous riots. The violent racial disturbances that erupted in Newark, New Jersey, and Detroit, Michigan, during the first two weeks in July 1967 were the costliest up to that point in American history. In hopes of defusing the rage expressed through these annual disturbances, President Lyndon Johnson assembled a panel, chaired by Illinois governor Otto Kerner, to examine the causes of and potential solutions to urban strife. On February 29, 1968, the Kerner Commission released a report claiming that white racism and institutionalized discrimination were root causes of poverty and violence in inner-city minority neighborhoods. Moreover, to prevent the "destruction of basic democratic values," the commission recommended massive federal intervention through increases in welfare, jobs, and low-income housing units.

President Johnson did not appreciate the alarmist tone of the Kerner report, and many white Americans rejected the notion that they were somehow responsible for race riots in the ghetto. Martin Luther King Jr., however, openly endorsed the report and announced that he would use its recommendations as the basis for a new social justice agenda. For more than a decade, the eloquent Baptist minister, civil rights advocate, and founding organizer of the Southern Christian Leadership Conference (SCLC) had implemented nonviolent strategies to confront racial segregation and discrimination in the South. By the late 1960s, King's political activism had expanded to include vocal opposition to the Vietnam War and support for a "Poor People's Campaign" that would seek to redistribute wealth through new federal programs for the impoverished. To the dismay of many in the Johnson administration, King drew connections between the violence in Vietnam and the mounting rage among poor urban blacks. Johnson's "War on Poverty," initiated in 1964, had been eclipsed by the war in Vietnam, argued King:

> We spend $322,000 for each enemy we kill, while we spend in the so-called war on poverty in America only about $53 for each person classified as "poor.". . . We must combine the fervor of the civil rights movement with the peace movement. We must demonstrate, teach, and preach until the very foundations of our nation are shaken.[1]

King's Assassination

In late March and early April 1968, King was in Memphis, Tennessee, to support a strike by its mostly black sanitation workers. In keeping with his decision to combine the struggle against racism with the struggle against poverty and war, he encouraged Memphis civil rights activists to embrace the grievances of the working poor as part of a larger campaign for human rights. "Let us develop a kind of dangerous unselfishness," he said during a speech at Memphis's Mason Street Temple on April 3. "Be concerned about your brother. You may not be on strike. But either we go up together, or we go down together." King, who was laying the groundwork for an upcoming march through Memphis, conceded that "We've got some difficult days ahead. But it doesn't matter with me now. . . . I've seen the promised land. I may not get there with you. But I want you to know tonight that we as a people will get to the promised land!"[2]

These final words of King's speech were eerily prophetic. The following day, as he stepped out onto a motel balcony, King was fatally shot. Within hours, riots broke out in more than one hundred American cities. From Washington, D.C., to Oakland, California, angry mobs of black Americans looted, committed acts of vandalism, and started fires in what *Newsweek* referred to as "the most widespread spasm of racial disorder"[3] in U.S. history. In a televised address from the White House, President Johnson tried to calm the nation, beseeching "all Americans . . . [to] search their hearts as they ponder this most tragic incident. . . . We can achieve nothing by lawlessness and divisiveness among the American people."[4] But many flatly rejected Johnson's plea for restraint. In Washington, D.C., Stokely Carmichael, a militant black organizer opposed to King's nonviolent stance, spoke before a crowd of hundreds: "Go home and get a gun!" he shouted. "When the white man comes he is coming to kill you. I don't want any black blood in the street. Go home and get you a gun and then come back because I got me a gun." At a news conference the day after the assassination, Carmichael stated that "when white America killed Dr. King . . . she declared war"[5] on black America. Roy Wilkins, executive director of the National Association for the Advancement of Colored People (NAACP), sharply rejected Carmichael's claims, mentioning that in all the "talk about 'Get Whitey' . . . the people who lose their lives are Negroes."[6] The facts proved Wilkins to be correct: Blacks constituted the majority of the more than forty deaths and hundreds of injuries that occurred in the five days of rioting.

Carmichael's angry exhortations did, however, convey the rage and bitterness felt by many African Americans of the time. Frustrated by the economic inequities and racism that continued despite the passage of federal civil rights laws, many city-dwelling blacks questioned the effectiveness of the nonviolent protest tactics espoused by King. Increasingly disillusioned with the idea of petitioning a white-dominated political system for basic human rights, some came to believe that justice could not be attained through peaceful confrontation and racial integration. They turned instead to a philosophy of self-defense and militant nationalism as a means to achieve black liberation. By 1968, several black nationalist groups had emerged, and most of them endorsed the possibility of using any means, even violence, to combat racial discrimination. The most famous of these militant groups, the Black Panthers, had initially formed with the intention of patrolling black neighborhoods to defend African Americans from police brutality. Their calls to unite black and white radicals in a revolutionary—and, if necessary, violent—struggle against racism and economic oppression appealed to young activists and college students of a more militant bent.

Robert Kennedy's Assassination

Those who continued to support less radical means of social change, however, looked to the presidential election of 1968. For many, Robert Kennedy, the Democratic senator from New York and brother of the late president John Kennedy, offered the strongest hope for effective leadership. Robert Kennedy had served in his brother's cabinet as U.S. attorney general from 1961 to 1963, and continued to hold the position under Johnson's presidency until 1964. During this time, he had unconditionally accepted John Kennedy's Vietnam policy, which emphasized the preservation of an independent South Vietnam against Communist incursion from the north. With Lyndon Johnson's presidency, this policy transformed into a deeper commitment: the deployment of U.S. combat troops to assist South Vietnam in its war against the northern Communist regime. As senator, Robert Kennedy initially supported Johnson's war strategy, believing that it was necessary to prevent communism from advancing in the developing world. Eventually, however, he broke with the Johnson administration, openly admitted that he had supported the wrong policy during his stint as attorney general, and argued for compromise and negotiation between North and South Vietnam. Early in 1968, after the North Vietnamese launched the Tet Offensive, a devastating surprise attack on South Vietnamese and U.S. military forces, public sentiment began to turn against the war. When Robert Kennedy announced his presidential candidacy in March 1968, he drew the support of many liberals and moderates who disapproved of Johnson's Vietnam policies.

Kennedy's apparent sincerity and candor—as well as the glamour and romance projected onto him through the public memory of his brother—broadened his appeal. He not only embodied the dynamism and optimism of his brother but exuded a vulnerability and compassion that attracted whites and minorities of all classes. On the day after the King assassination, Kennedy addressed the City Club of Cleveland, Ohio, denouncing the violence that had ended King's life and the violence that was erupting in cities across the country. He also spoke of

> another kind of violence, slower but just as deadly, destructive as the shot or the bomb in the night. This is the violence of institutions; indifference and inaction and slow decay. This is the violence that affects the poor, that poisons relations between men because their skin has different colors. This is a slow destruction of a child by hunger, and schools without books and homes without heat in the winter. . . . We must admit the vanity of our false distinctions. . . . Surely we can begin to work a little harder to bind up the wounds among us and to become in our own hearts brothers and countrymen again.[7]

Many analysts saw this speech as a turning point in Kennedy's presidential campaign—a move from a focus on denouncing the Vietnam War to a more expansive goal of racial reconciliation and economic justice. Supporters dreamed that a Robert Kennedy presidency might fill the cultural and political holes created by Johnson's failed policies and by the assassinations of John Kennedy and Martin Luther King. But this hope was not to be realized. On June 5, 1968, Kennedy was fatally shot in a Los Angeles hotel after delivering a campaign speech celebrating a primary election victory. The man arrested for Kennedy's assassination, Sirhan Sirhan, was a Jordanian immigrant who claimed to be upset over Kennedy's support of Israel.

In the midst of the profound sadness elicited by Kennedy's death, many people speculated that the assassination was part of a conspiracy orchestrated by radicals on the right or the left. As *Time* magazine reported in its June 14 issue, "Many found it difficult to believe that the assassinations of John Kennedy, Martin Luther King and Robert Kennedy were unrelated. Some blamed right-wing extremists; others concluded that all three slayings were part of a Communist plot to divide and weaken the U.S."[8]

Whether they were inclined or disinclined to believe in such conspiracy theories, Americans experienced a palpable anxiety concerning the incidents of violence and rage that were occurring with frightening regularity. Many feared that the country was on the verge of collapse, and they dreaded the unrest that the summer's presidential races might bring. Accordingly, one of the reasons President Johnson chose not to run for reelection in 1968 was concern over the turmoil that his campaigning might cause in major cities. Noting the increasing violence that was occurring during protests on college campuses, antiwar rallies, and antiestablishment demonstrations, some commentators blamed political dissenters for the chaos and called for stricter punishments of these activists.

The concerns about violence during the summer presidential campaigns turned out to be well founded, and the issue of rage itself became a deciding factor in the 1968 election. Independent candidate George M. Wallace, the former segregationist governor of Alabama, appealed to a segment of blue-collar whites who were disturbed by race riots and the federal government's insistence on integrating public schools. A critic of high taxes and liberal policies, Wallace promoted himself as a "law and order" candidate who would work to curb violence in the cities. Of wider appeal, however, was Republican candidate Richard M. Nixon, who had served as vice president under Dwight D. Eisenhower. Noting the shift in public opinion concerning the Vietnam War, Nixon skillfully modified his previous prowar stance and presented himself as a moderate who wished to find an honorable way to end the conflict. Most notably, however, he addressed the feelings of anxiety that were pervading the nation. In his acceptance speech at the Republican National Convention on August 8, 1968, he acknowledged that "We hear sirens in the night. We see Americans dying on distant battlefields abroad. We see Americans hating each other, fighting each other, killing each other at home." Then he spoke of the "quiet voice in the tumult of the shouting. It is the voice of the great majority of Americans, the non shouters, the non demonstrators." Nixon promised to answer the call of this silent majority by being tough on crime and on all perpetrators of violence. In doing so, he stated, "We shall re-establish freedom from fear in America so that America can take the lead of re-establishing freedom from fear in the world."[9]

A Riot in Chicago

Two weeks after Nixon's nomination speech, the Democratic National Convention opened in Chicago, Illinois. Several unsettling details regarding city security, as well as political differences within the Democratic Party, forecasted trouble for the week of events. For one thing, Chicago mayor Richard Daley, notorious for commanding city police to "shoot to kill arsonists and shoot to maim looters" in the wake of King's assassination, called out twelve thousand police officers, six thousand army troops, five thousand Illinois National Guardsmen, and one thousand secret servicemen to patrol the city. In an attempt to forestall potentially disruptive demonstrations, Daley also denied permits to various antiwar groups who had planned to stage protest marches and rallies. These groups felt drawn to protest at the Democrats' convention—rather than the Republicans'—because Democratic leaders had been responsible for the deployment of U.S. troops in Vietnam. The main groups who intended to make their presence known in Chicago included the National Mobilization to End the War in Vietnam (the "Mobe"); the Yippies, who wished to combine a countercultural "politics of ecstasy" with antiwar protest; and Students for a Democratic Society (SDS), a left-wing campus group.

The Democratic Party itself was deeply conflicted. The death of Robert Kennedy had left its antiwar contingent discouraged and divided. Party organizers attempted to develop a platform that would appeal to its liberal peace advocates as well as moderates and conservatives who backed Johnson's Vietnam policies. Vice President Hubert Humphrey seemed to be the candidate who might bridge differences among Democrats, as he had cautiously proposed an end to the bombing in North Vietnam and a negotiated withdrawal from the war. However, as the convention began, President Johnson insisted that the bombing could stop only "when this action would not endanger the lives of troops in the field."[10] Humphrey yielded to Johnson's declaration, and was thereafter perceived as a supporter of the war.

Mayor Daley's prohibition of demonstrations dissuaded many protesters from coming to the Chicago convention. Nevertheless, at least five thousand antiwar demonstrators gathered in Lincoln Park on the evening of August 25, the night before the convention began. While Mobe organizers urged the protesters to adhere to the 11:00 curfew, the Yippies encouraged confrontation. Nearly a thousand demonstrators defied orders to clear the park, and they clashed with about five hundred nightstick- and fist-wielding police officers. For the next two nights, as an additional five thousand demonstrators gathered, this scene intensified as police used clubs, tear gas, and gunfire to force the protesters out of the park.

The height of the violence occurred on Wednesday, August 28, following an approved rally in Grant Park, which was across the street from the Hilton Hotel where a number of delegates were staying. When someone appeared to be lowering an American flag near the center of the rally, police moved in and began beating demonstrators. The crowd responded by throwing bricks, rocks, and food at the police. Mobe organizer Rennie Davis was attacked when he attempted to restore order by stationing rally marshals between the protesters and police. Demonstrators eventually joined a legal march sponsored by the SCLC, which amassed a crowd of seven thousand in front of the Hilton Hotel. Police stormed this crowd, attacking protesters, reporters, and bystanders with clubs, mace, and fists. A British journalist reported that "the kids screamed and were beaten to the ground by cops who had completely lost their cool. Some of the policemen chanted, 'Kill, kill.'"[11] At the height of the melee, spectators were driven through the Hilton's plate-glass windows. Bleeding protesters yelled, "The whole world is watching!" Just as Humphrey received the Democrats' nomination for president, footage of this violent skirmish was televised. Hundreds were injured and arrested.

The Democrats left the convention with their party in utter disarray. Antiwar protesters and liberal Democrats had hoped that the public would sympathize with them, and that the actions of Daley and the Chicago police would expose the corruption and immorality of the established American political system. However, polls taken after the convention revealed that more than 70 percent of those surveyed supported the measures Daley had taken to maintain security. Many saw the demonstrators as troublesome lawbreakers who deserved the treatment they received. Most significantly, the rage in Chicago led many Americans to associate Democrats with lawlessness and disorder, the very vices that George Wallace and Richard Nixon had explicitly denounced. The Chicago riots ultimately boosted Nixon's ratings and helped him narrowly defeat Humphrey in November 1968.

Social analysts and historians have mixed views about the legacy of 1968. Some see it as the year that ushered in a new caution and cynicism about politics and political leaders. On the one hand, social justice advocates had seen their heroes assassinated, and antiestablishment protesters who had spilt their blood in the streets did not launch the revolution they had hoped for. On the other hand, the newly elected president, Nixon, would soon become infamous for his willingness to use illegal and unethical techniques to defeat his political opponents, and his resignation amid the Watergate scandal of the early 1970s would leave Americans with a distrust of government. Yet many observers of American culture retain a deep appreciation for 1968. Despite its rage and violence, 1968 is often remembered as the turning point in a decade that inspired people to demand civil rights, social change, economic justice, and personal freedom—ultimately making the United States a more tolerant, diverse, and democratic nation.

Notes

1. Quoted in Thomas Powers. *The War at Home.* New York: Grossman, 1973, pp. 160–61.
2. Martin Luther King Jr., speech delivered before the Mason Street Temple in Memphis, Tennessee, April 3, 1968.
3. *Newsweek*, April 15, 1968, p. 31.
4. Quoted in Jules Witcover, *The Year the Dream Died: Revisiting 1968 in America.* New York: Warner Books, 1997, p. 156.
5. Quoted in Witcover, *The Year the Dream Died*, p. 156.
6. Quoted in Witcover, *The Year the Dream Died*, p. 156.
7. Quoted in Witcover, *The Year the Dream Died*, p. 157.
8. *Time*, June 14, 1968, p. 20.
9. Richard M. Nixon, speech delivered before the Republican National Convention, Miami Beach, Florida, August 8, 1968.
10. Quoted in Lewis L. Gould, *1968: The Election That Changed America.* Chicago: Ivan R. Dee, 1993, p. 118.
11. Quoted in Gould, *1968*, p. 129.

Images of the Tet Offensive Hit Home

By Don Oberdorfer

North Vietnamese and Vietcong military forces launched a surprise attack throughout South Vietnam during the traditional Tet holiday in late January 1968. The Communist North apparently had hoped to spark a popular uprising against the South Vietnamese government and to discourage further U.S. military support of South Vietnam. By the end of March, the North Vietnamese had failed to achieve the goals of their Tet Offensive. However, as Don Oberdorfer explains in the following selection, televised images of destruction and death began to turn American public sentiment against the war. Moreover, on February 27, 1968, the CBS network aired a widely viewed news special in which a well-respected commentator, Walter Cronkite, pronounced his judgment against the war. Oberdorfer is a journalist and the author of *Tet!*, from which this selection is excerpted.

I n the United States, the shock and anger of the first days after Tet gave way to frustration and that in turn to a sense of futility and despair. With the intense and bloody fighting continuing and dramatic allied victories not in sight, many Americans began to reject the whole affair, to turn off and give up on the war. The fragile confidence of November [1967] had been shattered by the first shock wave and now even hope seemed to be fading. The oracles of American society, the commentators, editorial writers and leaders of private America, many of whom

Don Oberdorfer, *Tet!* New York: Doubleday, 1971. Copyright © 1971 by Don Oberdorfer. All rights reserved. Reproduced by permission.

had been uneasy and uncertain before, now became convinced
that the war was being lost or, at the very best, could not be won.
Those who had reached the same conclusion earlier now found
the final proof that their information and their hunches had been
right and that the government had been disastrously wrong. Their
attitude was "I told you so."

The government in Washington and the U.S. Command in
Saigon [South Vietnam], declared that the Communists had been
defeated, suffering unprecedented losses for which there was
nothing to show but propaganda. The officials, however, had
nothing much of their own to show to prove their case. No
Communist-dominated cities had been taken, territory seized or
captive peoples "liberated"—except for cities, territory and
people that had been counted in the government camp before the
Tet Offensive had begun. American and Vietnamese troops were
fighting to reclaim what they had lost, nothing more. The American government had previously relied on statistical indicators of
population and territorial security to prove "success," while the
dissenters had relied largely on intuition and intangibles: the attitudes of the Vietnamese people, the determination of the Viet
Cong, the limited effectiveness of American power in a civil war
in a faraway place. Now the tables were turned. The facts on the
ground argued that the Communists had achieved success, and
the indices of security showed a sharp deterioration in the Saigon
government's position. The U.S. Government argued that all this
was fleeting, but the argument rested on prediction, deduction
and intangibles. Beyond the claimed "body count" of the dead—
numbers which seemed then, as now, fantastic and unreasonable—there was little hard evidence for the government's case.

Television's Influence on Public Sentiment

The assertions of the President, his senior aides and the American military chiefs were more suspect than ever before. They had
sold success before, and Tet had proved the product faulty; the
public was not inclined to buy again. Communiqués and claims
had been devalued, words had lost their ability to persuade. It
seemed more than ever true that a picture was worth more than
ten thousand words, and a profusion of pictures with sound were
beamed into the nation's living rooms each evening. The twenty-
one-inch version was of the horror of a hotter war: battle action
throughout the country in early and mid-February [1968]; the

house-to-house fighting in Hue, which continued nearly all of February; the shelling, ground probes and forever "imminent" annnihilation of the surrounded Marines at Khe Sanh which went on through March; the ruined and smoking cities, visited one by one via the camera eye, revealing different nuances of destitution and destruction every time. . . .

Public opinion polls taken at the time registered wide swings in public attitudes about the war. The initial hawkishness of early February was followed by a wave of pessimism about the military position of the United States in late February. In mid-March the pollsters detected a decline in hawkishness to a level below that of any previous time and an upsurge in the number of Americans favoring a reduction in the U.S. military effort in Vietnam. For the first time, self-professed hawks in the public at large were outnumbered by self-professed doves. Gallup poll data suggests that nearly one person in every five switched from the hawk to the dove position between early February and the middle of March. It can be reasonably inferred that the television reflection of events was an important factor in the swing of public sentiment. . . .

During the Success Offensive the previous November, Gallup poll interviewers had asked the public, "Just your impression, do you think the U.S. and its allies are losing ground in Vietnam, standing still, or making progress?" The last week in February [1968] Gallup asked the same question again. The results:

	Nov. 1967	Feb. 1968
Losing	8%	23%
Standing still	33	38
Making progress	50	33
No opinion	9	6

The Conversion of Walter Cronkite

The government might lie and the generals exaggerate, the news might be unreal, the pictures posed or the sound dubbed in, but the kindly, businesslike man with the modest mustache was a person to be trusted. Five nights a week at 6:30 P.M. Walter Cronkite put his well-worn pipe aside, picked up his script and recounted the day's events to a nation of viewers. Whenever there was a national crisis or a superstory, when a presidential candidate was nominated, a President elected or a President killed, when astronauts hurtled into space or returned to earth, Cronkite was there on the home screen, presiding over the telling of it all.

The *CBS Evening News* with Walter Cronkite was the first and most consistently popular half-hour nightly news program. President John F. Kennedy inaugurated the first edition on September 2, 1963, with an exclusive interview which expressed his displeasure at President [Ngo Dinh] Diem of South Vietnam, and played a role in triggering Diem's fall from power. Then and thereafter the Cronkite show was a coveted forum for politicians and statesmen and others seeking the eye and ear of the country. Pollster John Kraft, hired by the AFL-CIO Committee on Political Education to investigate the opinions of rank-and-file union members in January 1967, reported that 47 per cent of those polled said television was their most reliable source of information, and by far the most popular television newsman was Walter Cronkite. Chairman John Bailey of the Democratic National Committee took a close look at labor's findings, and told a Democratic Party conference, "What I'm afraid this means is that by a mere inflection of his deep baritone voice or by a lifting of his well-known bushy eyebrows, Cronkite might well change the vote of thousands of people around the country. . . . With the vast power he obviously holds over the nationwide audience, I hope he never becomes too uhappy with my candidate."

In early 1968 Cronkite became mightily unhappy with Chairman Bailey's candidate, Lyndon B. Johnson, and with the candidate's war. After Tet, Cronkite went to Vietnam to see what was going on and returned with a judgment against the war. Coming from a man who rarely expressed strong opinions on any controversial subject, the impact of this conversion was substantial. Presidential Press Secretary George Christian said later that when Walter Cronkite announced his post-Tet stand, "the shock waves rolled through the government." They rolled through the American body politic as well.

Not a Pacifist

Cronkite had been an illustrious United Press correspondent in World War II, landing with the Allied troops in North Africa and at Normandy beachhead, dropping from the skies with the 101st Airborne Division into Holland, participating in the first B-17 mission over Germany, breaking out of the German encirclement at Bastogne with the Third Army in the Battle of the Bulge. He was anything but a pacifist and like most Americans he was inclined to approve the purposes and policies of the United States in its postwar struggle with the Communist world.

Cronkite is one of the few television news stars with long experience as a newspaper or wire service reporter, and he thinks of himself as a reporter rather than a pundit. When the Vietnam War began to heat up in mid-1965, he went out to take a look and was impressed with the extent and purpose of the American undertaking. He was told that for the first time, the United States was trying to build a nation while fighting a war on foreign soil, instead of fighting and destroying and rebuilding later as in World War II. In view of the positive objective, Cronkite could understand and accept the limits on the use of American military power, and he had no doubt that this was a long-term engagement. After returning from Vietnam he praised "the courageous decision that Communism's advance must be stopped in Asia and that guerrilla war as a means to a political end must be finally discouraged." In the introduction to a book of CBS broadcasts about the nature of the war, Cronkite declared, "this is the meaning of our commitment in Southeast Asia—a commitment not for this year or next year but, more likely, for a generation. This is the way it must be if we are to fulfill our pledge to ourselves and to others to stop Communist aggression wherever it raises its head."

In 1966 and 1967 he was troubled by reports from the war zone and by the growing opposition to the war among colleagues he respected. He was reassured by government officials, who said the reporters were wrong. He was called to Washington three times by President Johnson for private meetings and briefed by senior officials. "They kept saying there was light at the end of the tunnel," he recalled later—but somehow it never dawned. Cronkite was shocked by the first news of the Tet Offensive and fed up with the contradiction between the official reports and the news reports from the war zone. He decided he owed it to the people who watched him every night to find out what was going on and let them know point-blank in a personal report. After consulting the CBS front office, he flew to Vietnam. An hour-long CBS News special was planned for his return.

Cronkite's Tour of Vietnam

He arrived in Saigon February 11, [1968], and saw the deserted streets and smelled the stench of garbage, which reminded him

A South Vietnamese soldier directs refugees past the bodies of North Vietnamese soldiers during the Tet Offensive.

of home—in New York, a garbage strike was under way. After dinner, somebody took him to the Caravelle roof to watch the war five or six miles away. After a tour of Saigon and interviews with the U.S. generals, he reported in a filmed summary from the Caravelle roof that "the Viet Cong suffered a military defeat" but that on the other hand, "the Tet Offensive has widened a credibility gap which exists here too between what the people are told and what they see about them."

The veteran war reporter toured the country to inspect the damage, and was astounded to hear military officers and pacification advisers claim victory for the government side. Cronkite flew to Hue while the battle there still raged. He donned a steel helmet and a flak jacket, slept on the floor of a Vietnamese doctor's house commandeered as a press center, ate C rations, sucked his pipe and took a close look at the Marines at war. The more he looked, the more it reminded him of Europe in World War II, and the less relevant it seemed to the original conception of a struggle to build a nation.

He spent an evening at nearby Phu Bai, where General

Creighton Abrams, the U.S. deputy commander, had established a forward headquarters. Cronkite had known him as Colonel Abrams of the 4th Armored Division at the Battle of the Bulge, and the two men were at ease with one another. In the commentator's presence, Abrams and other senior officers sat around a fireplace in the general's quarters at Phu Bai mulling the deployment of task forces and separate battalions, speaking of pincers movements, blocking forces and air strikes and drawing blue arrows on the battle maps. "It was sickening to me," Cronkite recalled later. "They were talking strategy and tactics with no consideration of the bigger job of pacifying and restoring the country. This had come to be total war, not a counterinsurgency or an effort to get the North Vietnamese out so we could support the indigenous effort. This was a World War II battlefield. The ideas I had talked about in 1965 were gone."

On the long plane ride home Cronkite and his producer, Ernest Leiser, worked on the details of their news special, reviewing the footage which had been shot and the conclusions which had been reached. After arriving in New York, they were disturbed to learn that the planned one-hour show had been shaved to thirty minutes. Cronkite and Leiser argued in vain for more time. When they were unsuccessful, they decided to use the best of their leftover footage for a series of short, hard-hitting reports on the regular 6:30 P.M. *Evening News.*

The Only Realistic Conclusion

The half-hour CBS News special, *Report from Vietnam by Walter Cronkite*, went on the air at 10 P.M. on February 27, and according to the Nielsen rating service, some nine million Americans were watching. Beginning with an introductory statement amid the rubble of a blasted street in Saigon, Cronkite showed films of the action and its aftermath and alternating interviews with optimistic and pessimistic Vietnamese and Americans. After the final station break, he confronted the camera from behind a desk in New York to deliver his personal assessment, labeled as such.

Who won and who lost in the great Tet Offensive against the cities? I'm not sure. The Viet Cong did not win by a knockout, but neither did we. The referees of history may make it a draw. Another standoff may be coming in the big battle expected south of the Demilitarized Zone. Khe Sanh could well fall with a terrible loss of American lives, prestige and morale, and this is a tragedy of our stubbornness there: but the bastion is no longer a key to the rest of the northern regions and it is doubtful that the American forces can be defeated across the breadth of the DMZ [Demilitarized Zone] with any substantial loss of ground. Another standoff. On the political front, past performance gives no confidence that the Vietnamese government can cope with its problems, now compounded by the attack on the cities. It may not fall, it may hold on, but probably won't show the dynamic qualities demanded of this young nation. Another standoff.

. . . It seems now more certain than ever that the bloody experience of Vietnam is to end in a stalemate. This summer's almost certain standoff will either end in real give-and-take negotiations or terrible escalation; and for every means we have to escalate, the enemy can match us, and that applies to invasion of the North, the use of nuclear weapons, or the mere commitment of one hundred or two hundred or three hundred thousand more American troops to the battle. And with each escalation, the world comes close to the brink of cosmic disaster.

To say that we are closer to victory today is to believe, in the face of the evidence, the optimists who have been wrong in the past. To suggest we are on the edge of defeat is to yield to unreasonable pessimism. To say that we are mired in stalemate seems the only realistic, yet unsatisfactory, conclusion.

On the off chance that military and political analysts are right, in the next months we must test the enemy's intentions in case this is indeed his last big gasp before negotiations. But it is increasingly clear to this reporter that the only rational way out then will be to negotiate, not as victors but as an honorable people who lived up to their pledge to defend democracy, and did the best they could.

This is Walter Cronkite. Good night.

The Kerner Commission Report

By the National Advisory Commission on Civil Disorders

In response to several devastating race riots during the summer of 1967, President Lyndon Johnson convened a government commission, chaired by Illinois governor Otto Kerner, to examine the causes and potential solutions to such civil disturbances. On February 29, 1968, the commission issued a report on its findings, claiming that white racism and institutionalized discrimination were the root causes of frustration and violence in the inner city. To prevent further racial division, the commission argues, well-funded programs must be established to enhance opportunities and foster hope among minorities and the poor. The following selection is excerpted from the introduction to the Kerner Report.

T he summer of 1967 again brought racial disorders to American cities, and with them shock, fear and bewilderment to the nation.

The worst came during a two-week period in July, first in Newark and then in Detroit. Each set off a chain reaction in neighboring communities.

On July 28, 1967, the President of the United States established this Commission and directed us to answer three basic questions:
- What happened?
- Why did it happen?

National Advisory Commission on Civil Disorders, *Kerner Commission Report of 1968*, February 1968.

• What can be done to prevent it from happening again?

To respond to these questions, we have undertaken a broad range of studies and investigations. We have visited the riot cities; we have heard many witnesses; we have sought the counsel of experts across the country.

Deepening Divisions

This is our basic conclusion: Our nation is moving toward two societies, one black, one white—separate and unequal.

Reaction to last summer's disorders has quickened the movement and deepened the division. Discrimination and segregation have long permeated much of American life; they now threaten the future of every American.

This deepening racial division is not inevitable. The movement apart can be reversed. Choice is still possible. Our principal task is to define that choice and to press for a national resolution.

To pursue our present course will involve the continuing polarization of the American community and, ultimately, the destruction of basic democratic values.

The alternative is not blind repression or capitulation to lawlessness. It is the realization of common opportunities for all within a single society.

This alternative will require a commitment to national action—compassionate, massive and sustained, backed by the resources of the most powerful and the richest nation on this earth. From every American it will require new attitudes, new understanding, and, above all, new will.

The vital needs of the nation must be met; hard choices must be made, and, if necessary, new taxes enacted.

The Violence Must End

Violence cannot build a better society. Disruption and disorder nourish repression, not justice. They strike at the freedom of every citizen. The community cannot—it will not—tolerate coercion and mob rule.

Violence and destruction must be ended—in the streets of the ghetto and in the lives of people.

Segregation and poverty have created in the racial ghetto a destructive environment totally unknown to most white Americans.

What white Americans have never fully understood—but what the Negro can never forget—is that white society is deeply implicated in the ghetto. White institutions created it, white institutions maintain it, and white society condones it.

Strategies for Action

It is time now to turn with all the purpose at our command to the major unfinished business of this nation. It is time to adopt strategies for action that will produce quick and visible progress. It is time to make good the promises of American democracy to all citizens—urban and rural, white and black, Spanish-surname, American Indian, and every minority group.

Our recommendations embrace three basic principles:

- To mount programs on a scale equal to the dimension of the problems;
- To aim these programs for high impact in the immediate future in order to close the gap between promise and performance;
- To undertake new initiatives and experiments that can change the system of failure and frustration that now dominates the ghetto and weakens our society.

These programs will require unprecedented levels of funding and performance, but they neither probe deeper nor demand more than the problems which called them forth. There can be no higher priority for national action and no higher claim on the nation's conscience.

We issue this Report now, four months before the date called for by the President. Much remains that can be learned. Continued study is essential.

As Commissioners we have worked together with a sense of the greatest urgency and have sought to compose whatever differences exist among us. Some differences remain. But the gravity of the problem and the pressing need for action are too clear to allow further delay in the issuance of this Report.

I See the Promised Land: Martin Luther King Jr.'s Final Speech

By Martin Luther King Jr.

In 1957 Baptist minister Martin Luther King Jr. founded the Southern Christian Leadership Conference (SCLC), a civil rights organization that challenged racial segregation through a combined strategy of nonviolent direct action, litigation, boycotts, and voter registration. The following selection is a speech he delivered before a gathering of civil rights supporters in Memphis, Tennessee, on April 3, 1968—just one day before his assassination. King had come to Memphis to support the city's sanitation workers, who were on strike. He encourages activists to develop a "dangerous unselfishness," that is, to continue the struggle for human rights by confronting injustices that may not affect them personally, such as unfair labor policies. King also expresses deep gratitude for being alive during a time of tremendous change and civil rights advances for black Americans.

T hank you very kindly, my friends. . . .
I'm delighted to see each of you here tonight in spite of a storm warning. You reveal that you are determined to go on anyhow. Something is happening in Memphis, something is happening in our world.

Martin Luther King Jr., speech delivered at the Mason Street Temple in Memphis, Tennessee, April 3, 1968. Copyright © 1968 by Dr. Martin Luther King Jr. Renewed in 1991 by Coretta Scott King. Reproduced by arrangement with the Estate of Martin Luther King Jr., c/o Writers House Inc. as agent for the proprietor, New York, NY.

As you know, if I were standing at the beginning of time, with the possibility of general and panoramic view of the whole human history up to now, and the Almighty said to me, "Martin Luther King, which age would you like to live in?"—I would take my mental flight by Egypt through, or rather across the Red Sea, through the wilderness on toward the promised land. And in spite of its magnificence, I wouldn't stop there. I would move on by Greece, and take my mind to Mount Olympus. And I would see Plato, Aristotle, Socrates, Euripides and Aristophanes assembled around the Parthenon as they discussed the great and eternal issues of reality.

But I wouldn't stop there. I would go on, even to the great heyday of the Roman Empire. And I would see developments around there, through various emperors and leaders. But I wouldn't stop there. I would even come up to the day of the Renaissance, and get a quick picture of all that the Renaissance did for the cultural and esthetic life of man. But I wouldn't stop there. I would even go by the way that the man for whom I'm named had his habitat. And I would watch Martin Luther as he tacked his ninety-five theses on the door at the church in Wittenberg.

But I wouldn't stop there. I would come on up even to 1863, and watch a vacillating president by the name of Abraham Lincoln finally come to the conclusion that he had to sign the Emancipation Proclamation. But I wouldn't stop there. I would even come up to the early thirties, and see a man grappling with the problems of the bankruptcy of his nation. And come with an eloquent cry that we have nothing to fear but fear itself.

But I wouldn't stop there. Strangely enough, I would turn to the Almighty, and say, "If you allow me to live just a few years in the second half of the twentieth century, I will be happy." Now that's a strange statement to make, because the world is all messed up. The nation is sick. Trouble is in the land. Confusion all around. That's a strange statement. But I know, somehow, that only when it is dark enough, can you see the stars. And I see God working in this period of the twentieth century in a way that men, in some strange way, are responding—something is happening in our world. The masses of people are rising up. And wherever they are assembled today, whether they are in Johannesburg, South Africa; Nairobi, Kenya; Accra, Ghana; New York City; Atlanta, Georgia; Jackson, Mississippi; or Memphis, Tennessee—the cry is always the same—"We want to be free."

The Need to Maintain Unity

And another reason that I'm happy to live in this period is that we have been forced to a point where we're going to have to grapple with the problems that men have been trying to grapple with through history, but the demands didn't force them to do it. Survival demands that we grapple with them. Men, for years now, have been talking about war and peace. But now, no longer can they just talk about it. It is no longer a choice between violence and nonviolence in this world; it's nonviolence or nonexistence.

That is where we are today. And also in the human rights revolution, if something isn't done, and in a hurry, to bring the colored peoples of the world out of their long years of poverty, their long years of hurt and neglect, the whole world is doomed. Now, I'm just happy that God has allowed me to live in this period, to see what is unfolding. And I'm happy that he's allowed me to be in Memphis.

I can remember, I can remember when Negroes were just going around . . . scratching where they didn't itch, and laughing when they were not tickled. But that day is all over. We mean business now, and we are determined to gain our rightful place in God's world.

And that's all this whole thing is about. We aren't engaged in any negative protest and in any negative arguments with anybody. We are saying that we are determined to be men. We are determined to be people. We are saying that we are God's children. And that we don't have to live like we are forced to live.

Now, what does all of this mean in this great period of history? It means that we've got to stay together. We've got to stay together and maintain unity. You know, whenever Pharaoh wanted to prolong the period of slavery in Egypt, he had a favorite, favorite formula for doing it. What was that? He kept the slaves fighting among themselves. But whenever the slaves get together, something happens in Pharaoh's court, and he cannot hold the slaves in slavery. When the slaves get together, that's the beginning of getting out of slavery. Now let us maintain unity.

Injustice Is the Issue

Secondly, let us keep the issues where they are. The issue is injustice. The issue is the refusal of Memphis to be fair and honest in its dealings with its public servants, who happen to be sanitation workers. Now, we've got to keep attention on that. That's always the problem with a little violence. You know what happened the other day, and the press dealt only with the window-breaking. I read the articles. They very seldom got around to mentioning the fact that one thousand, three hundred sanitation workers were on strike, and that Memphis is not being fair to them, and that Mayor Loeb is in dire need of a doctor. They didn't get around to that.

Now we're going to march again, and we've got to march again, in order to put the issue where it is supposed to be. And force everybody to see that there are thirteen hundred of God's children here suffering, sometimes going hungry, going through dark and dreary nights wondering how this thing is going to come out. That's the issue. And we've got to say to the nation: we know it's coming out. For when people get caught up with that which is right and they are willing to sacrifice for it, there is no stopping point short of victory.

We aren't going to let any mace stop us. We are masters in our nonviolent movement in disarming police forces; they don't know what to do. I've seen them so often. I remember in Birmingham, Alabama, when we were in that majestic struggle there we would move out of the 16th Street Baptist Church day after day; by the hundreds we would move out. And [Police Chief] Bull Connor would tell them to send the dogs forth and they did come; but we just went before the dogs singing, "Ain't gonna let nobody turn me round." Bull Connor next would say, "Turn the fire hoses on." And as I said to you the other night, Bull Connor didn't know history. He knew a kind of physics that somehow didn't relate to the transphysics that we knew about. And that was the fact that there was a certain kind of fire that no water could put out. And we went before the fire hoses; we had known water. If we were Baptist or some other denomination, we had been immersed. If we were Methodist, and some others, we had been sprinkled, but we knew water.

That couldn't stop us. And we just went on before the dogs and we would look at them; and we'd go on before the water hoses and we would look at it, and we'd just go on singing. "Over my head I see freedom in the air." And then we would be thrown in the paddy wagons, and sometimes we were stacked in there like sardines in a can. And they would throw us in, and old Bull would say, "Take them off," and they did; and we would just go in the paddy wagon singing, "We Shall Overcome." And every now and then we'd get in the jail, and we'd see the jailers looking through the windows being moved by our prayers, and being moved by our words and our songs. And there was a power there which Bull Connor couldn't adjust to; and so we ended up transforming Bull into a steer, and we won our struggle in Birmingham.

What Must Be Done

Now we've got to go on to Memphis just like that. I call upon you to be with us Monday. Now about injunctions: We have an injunction and we're going into court tomorrow morning to fight this illegal, unconstitutional injunction. All we say to America is, "Be true to what you said on paper." If I lived in China or even Russia, or any totalitarian country, maybe I could understand the denial of certain basic First Amendment privileges, because they hadn't committed themselves to that over there. But somewhere I read of the freedom of assembly. Somewhere I read of the freedom of speech. Somewhere I read of the freedom of the press. Somewhere I read that the greatness of America is the right to protest for right. And so just as I say, we aren't going to let any injunction turn us around. We are going on.

We need all of you. And you know what's beautiful to me, is to see all of these ministers of the Gospel. It's a marvelous picture. Who is it that is supposed to articulate the longings and aspirations of the people more than the preacher? Somehow the preacher must be an Amos, and say, "Let justice roll down like waters and righteousness like a mighty stream," Somehow, the preacher must say with Jesus, "The spirit of the Lord is upon me, because he hath anointed me to deal with the problems of the poor." . . .

It's alright to talk about "long white robes over yonder," in all of its symbolism. But ultimately people want some suits and dresses and shoes to wear down here. It's alright to talk about "streets flowing with milk and honey," but God has commanded us to be concerned about the slums down here, and his children who can't eat three square meals a day. It's alright to talk about the new Jerusalem, but one day, God's preacher must talk about the New York, the new Atlanta, the new Philadelphia, the new Los Angeles, the new Memphis, Tennessee. This is what we have to do.

Economic Action

Now the other thing we'll have to do is this: Always anchor our external direct action with the power of economic withdrawal.

Now, we are poor people, individually, we are poor when you compare us with white society in America. We are poor. Never stop and forget that collectively, that means all of us together, collectively we are richer than all the nations in the world, with the exception of nine. Did you ever think about that? After you leave the United States, Soviet Russia, Great Britain, West Germany, France, and I could name the others, the Negro collectively is richer than most nations of the world. We have an annual income of more than thirty billion dollars a year, which is more than all of the exports of the United States, and more than the national budget of Canada. Did you know that? That's power right there, if we know how to pool it.

We don't have to argue with anybody. We don't have to curse and go around acting bad with our words. We don't need any bricks and bottles, we don't need any Molotov cocktails, we just need to go around to these stores, and to these massive industries in our country, and say, "God sent us by here, to say to you that you're not treating his children right. And we've come by here to ask you to make the first item on your agenda—fair treatment, where God's children are concerned. Now, if you are not pre-

Martin Luther King Jr. speaks to a crowd in Selma, Alabama. He encouraged civil rights activists to fight for all human rights.

pared to do that, we do have an agenda that we must follow. And our agenda calls for withdrawing economic support from you."

And so, as a result of this, we are asking you tonight, to go out and tell your neighbors not to buy Coca-Cola in Memphis. Go by and tell them not to buy Sealtest milk. Tell them not to buy—what is the other bread?—Wonder Bread. And what is the other bread company, Jesse? Tell them not to buy Hart's bread. As Jesse Jackson has said, up to now, only the garbage men have been feeling pain; now we must kind of redistribute the pain. We are choosing these companies because they haven't been fair in their hiring policies; and we are choosing them because they can begin the process of saying they are going to support the needs and the rights of these men who are on strike. And then they can move on downtown and tell Mayor Loeb to do what is right. . . .

Struggle Until the End

Now, let me say as I move to my conclusion that we've got to give ourselves to this struggle until the end. Nothing would be more tragic than to stop at this point, in Memphis. We've got to see it through. And when we have our march, you need to be there. Be concerned about your brother. You may not be on strike. But either we go up together, or we go down together.

Let us develop a kind of dangerous unselfishness. One day a man came to Jesus; and he wanted to raise some questions about some vital matters in life. At points, he wanted to trick Jesus, and show him that he knew a little more than Jesus knew, and through this, throw him off base. Now that question could have easily ended up in a philosophical and theological debate. But Jesus immediately pulled that question from mid-air, and placed it on a dangerous curve between Jerusalem and Jericho. And he talked about a certain man who fell among thieves. You remember that a Levite and a priest passed by on the other side. They didn't stop to help him. And finally a man of another race came by. He got down from his beast, decided not to be compassionate by proxy. But [he] administered first aid and helped the man in need. Jesus ended up saying this was the good man, because he had the capacity to project the "I" into the "thou," and to be concerned about his brother. Now you know, we use our imagination a great deal to try to determine why the priest and the Levite didn't stop. At times we say they were busy going to church meetings—an ecclesiastical gathering—and they had to get on down to Jerusalem so they wouldn't be late for their meeting. At other times we would speculate that there was a religious law that "One who was engaged in religious ceremonials was not to touch a human body twenty-four hours before the ceremony." And every now and then we begin to wonder whether maybe they were not going down to Jerusalem, or down to Jericho, rather to organize a "Jericho Road Improvement Association." That's a possibility. Maybe they felt that it was better to deal with the problem from the causal root, rather than to get bogged down with an individual effort.

But I'm going to tell you what my imagination tells me. It's possible that these men were afraid. You see, the Jericho road is a dangerous road. I remember when Mrs. King and I were first in Jerusalem. We rented a car and drove from Jerusalem down to Jericho. And as soon as we got on that road, I said to my wife, "I can see why Jesus used this as a setting for his parable." It's a winding, meandering road. It's really conducive for ambushing. You start out in Jerusalem, which is about 1200 miles, or rather 1200 feet above sea level. And by the time you get down to Jericho, fifteen or twenty minutes later, you're about 2200 feet below sea level. That's a dangerous road. In the day of Jesus it came to be known as the "Bloody Pass." And you know, it's possible that the priest and the Levite looked over that man on the ground and wondered if the robbers were still around. Or it's possible that they felt that the man on the ground was merely faking. And he was acting like he had been robbed and hurt, in order to seize them over there, lure them there for quick and easy seizure. And so the first question that the Levite asked was, "if I stop to help this man, what will happen to me?" But then the Good Samaritan came by. And he reversed the question: "If I do not stop to help this man, what will happen to him?"

That's the question before you tonight. Not, "If I stop to help the sanitation workers, what will happen to all of the hours that I usually spend in my office every day and every week as a pastor?" The question is not, "If I stop to help this man in need, what will happen to me?" "If I do no stop to held the sanitation workers, what will happen to them?" That's the question.

A Greater Determination

Let us rise up tonight with a greater readiness. Let us stand with a greater determination. And let us move on in these powerful days, these days of challenge to make America what it ought to be. We have an opportunity to make America a better nation. And I want to thank God, once more, for allowing me to be here with you.

You know, several years ago, I was in New York City autographing the first book that I had written. And while sitting there autographing books, a demented black woman came up. The only question I heard from her was, "Are you Martin Luther King?"

And I was looking down writing, and I said yes. And the next minute I felt something beating on my chest. Before I knew it I had been stabbed by this demented woman. I was rushed to Harlem Hospital. It was a dark Saturday afternoon. And that blade had gone through, and the X-rays revealed that the tip of the blade was on the edge of my aorta, the main artery. And once that's punctured, you drown in your own blood—that's the end of you.

It came out in the *New York Times* the next morning, that if I had sneezed, I would have died. Well, about four days later, they allowed me, after the operation, after my chest had been opened, and the blade had been taken out, to move around in the wheel chair in the hospital. They allowed me to read some of the mail that came in, and from all over the states, and the world, kind letters came in. I read a few, but one of them I will never forget. I had received one from the President and the Vice-President. I've forgotten what those telegrams said. I'd received a visit and a letter from the Governor of New York, but I've forgotten what the letter said. But there was another letter that came from a little girl, a young girl who was a student at the White Plains High School. And I looked at that letter, and I'll never forget it. It said simply, "Dear Dr. King: I am a ninth-grade student at the Whites Plains High School." She said, "While it should not matter, I would like to mention that I am a white girl. I read in the paper of your misfortune, and of your suffering. And I read that if you had sneezed, you would have died. And I'm simply writing you to say that I'm so happy that you didn't sneeze."

And I want to say tonight, I want to say that I am happy that I didn't sneeze. Because if I had sneezed, I wouldn't have been around here in 1960, when students all over the South started sitting-in at lunch counters. And I knew that as they were sitting in, they were really standing up for the best in the American dream. And taking the whole nation back to those great wells of democracy which were dug deep by the Founding Fathers in the Declaration of Independence and the Constitution. If I had sneezed, I wouldn't have been around in 1962, when Negroes in Albany, Georgia, decided to straighten their backs up. And whenever men and women straighten their backs up, they are going somewhere, because a man can't ride your back unless it is bent. If I had sneezed, I wouldn't have been here in 1963, when the black people of Birmingham, Alabama, aroused the conscience of this nation, and brought into being the Civil Rights Bill. If I had sneezed, I wouldn't have had a chance later that year, in August, to try to tell America about a dream that I had had. If I had sneezed, I wouldn't have been down in Selma, Alabama, to see the great movement there. If I had sneezed, I wouldn't have been in Memphis to see a community rally around those brothers and sisters who are suffering. I'm so happy that I didn't sneeze.

The Mountaintop

And they were telling me . . . , it doesn't matter now. It really doesn't matter what happens now. I left Atlanta this morning, and as we got started on the plane, there were six of us, the pilot said over the public address system, "We are sorry for the delay, but we have Dr. Martin Luther King on the plane. And to be sure that all of the bags were checked, and to be sure that nothing would be wrong with the plane, we had to check out everything carefully. And we've had the plane protected and guarded all night."

And then I got into Memphis. And some began to say that threats, or talk about the threats that were out. What would happen to me from some of our sick white brothers?

Well, I don't know what will happen now. We've got some difficult days ahead. But it doesn't matter with me now. Because I've been to the mountaintop. And I don't mind. Like anybody, I would like to live a long life. Longevity has its place. But I'm not concerned about that now. I just want to do God's will. And He's allowed me to go up to the mountain. And I've looked over. And I've seen the promised land. I may not get there with you. But I want you to know tonight, that we as a people will get to the promised land. And I'm happy tonight. I'm not worried about anything. I'm not fearing any man. Mine eyes have seen the glory of the coming of the Lord!

Take Everything You Need, Baby

By *Newsweek*

On April 4, 1968, civil rights leader Martin Luther King Jr. was fatally shot as he stood on a motel balcony in Memphis, Tennessee. As a result, from April 5 through April 9, riots occurred in 125 U.S. cities, leaving at least forty dead and hundreds injured. The following article from *Newsweek* recounts some details from the civil disturbances in Washington, D.C.; Chicago, Illinois; and New York City. Washington and Chicago were especially hard hit, reports *Newsweek*, as crowds of outraged blacks—many of them teenagers—firebombed, vandalized, and looted the inner cities. Thousands of army and National Guard troops were called in to restore order.

I t was Pandora's box flung open—an apocalyptic act that loosed the furies brooding in the shadows of America's sullen ghettos. From Washington to Oakland, Tallahassee to Denver, the murder of Martin Luther King Jr. in Memphis last week touched off a black rampage that subjected the U.S. to the most widespread spasm of racial disorder in its violent history.

The fire this time made Washington look like the besieged capital of a banana republic with helmeted combat troops, bayoneted rifles at the ready, guarding the White House and a light-machine-gun post defending the steps of the Capitol. Huge sections of Chicago's West Side ghetto were put to the torch. The National Guard was called out there and in Detroit, Pittsburgh,

"Take Everything You Need, Baby," *Newsweek*, April 15, 1968, pp. 31–34. Copyright © 1968 by Newsweek, Inc. All rights reserved. Reproduced by permission.

Baltimore and in four Southern cities, and put on alert in Philadelphia and Boston. In New York, Mayor John V. Lindsay was heckled from a Harlem street by an angry crowd. In Minneapolis, a Negro vowed to kill the first honky he saw—and promptly shot his white neighbor to death. "My King is dead," he sobbed, after pumping half a dozen bullets into his victim.

Negro college campuses seethed with anger and sometimes harbored snipers. Dozens of high schools canceled classes after violence erupted between Negro and white students. Window-breaking, rock-throwing, looting and other acts of vandalism struck two score cities, large and small. Washington, Chicago, Detroit and Toledo tried to enforce dusk-to-dawn curfews. Bars, liquor stores and gun shops were closed in many places—but usually not before ghetto blacks had stocked up on alcohol and ammunition. Throughout the country, already-overburdened police and firemen went on emergency shifts. By the weekend, the death toll around the U.S. stood at more than twenty and was rising, uncounted thousands were under arrest (more than 4,000 in Washington alone) and property damage was incalculable.

King's assassination was quite clearly the proximate cause of it all—but the rioters' anger and grief was often hard to detect. The Chicago mobs were ugly and obviously well schooled in the use of fire bombs. But in Washington the looters had a Mardi Gras air about them. Around the country, whites were jeered, threatened and occasionally assaulted, but the crowds generally avoided confrontations with the police. The police, too, did their best to keep bloodshed at a minimum. Indeed, in city after city, the cops were under orders not to interfere with looting. And it was quite apparent that the rioters' main target was to loot, not shoot honkies. "Soul Brother" signs afforded Negro business-men little of the protection they assured in past riots. The plun-derers—led by black teen-agers—smashed and burned almost indiscriminately.

"Guns"

Washington, which is 66 per cent Negro but which had been al-most untouched by the last four riotous summers, was the hard-est hit this time. Minutes after the news of King's death was broadcast, crowds began to gather on the edges of the Capital's sprawling ghettos. They did not have to wait long for a leader. Into the volatile mix swept black power-monger Stokely

Carmichael spouting incendiary rhetoric. "Go home and get your guns," cried Carmichael. "When the white man comes he is coming to kill you. I don't want any black blood in the street. Go home and get you a gun and then come back because I got me a gun"—and he brandished what looked like a small pistol.

Roving bands of black teen-agers—unarmed so far as anyone could tell—were already darting into Washington's downtown shopping district, fires were beginning to light the night sky and Washington's relatively small (2,900-man) police force went on the alert. The plundering and burning lasted until dawn, then subsided—only to resume with far greater intensity next day.

Friday was a crisp spring day in the Capital. The cherry blossoms were in bloom and the city was thronged with tourists who gawked in amazement through the tinted windows of their sightseeing buses as the rampage resumed.

The Frisk

At his storefront headquarters, Stokely Carmichael helped feed the flames with more violent talk—all of it delivered in a soft, gentle voice to newsmen (who were frisked and relieved of such potential weapons as nail clippers before being admitted to his presence). "When white America killed Dr. King," said Carmichael, who bitterly opposed King's nonviolent stance, "she declared war on us. . . . We have to retaliate for the deaths of our leaders. The executions of those deaths [are] going to be in the streets. . . ." Did Carmichael, 27, fear for his own life? "The hell with my life," he snapped at a white reporter. "You should fear for yours. I know I'm going to die." Later, he turned up at a memorial service for King at Howard University, waving a gun on the platform.

As the day wore on, the turmoil increased. Looting and burning swept down 14th Street and 7th Street, two of the ghetto's main thoroughfares, then spread south to the shopping district just east of the White House. On the sidewalk in front of the Justice Department's headquarters on Pennsylvania Avenue, shirt-sleeved DOJ staffers watched helplessly as looters cleaned out Kaufman's clothing store. The story was the same all over. Without the force to control the situation, the cops let the looters run wild. The result was an eerie, carnival atmosphere. Jolly blacks dashed in and out of shattered shopwindows carrying their booty away in plain sight of the law. Others tooled through the shopping districts in late-model cars, pausing to fill them with loot and then speeding off—only to stop obediently for red lights.

Looters stopped on the sidewalks to try on new sports jackets and to doff their old shoes for stolen new ones. Only rarely did police interfere. At the corner of 14th and G Streets, police braced a Negro over a car. On the hood were several pairs of shoes. "They killed my brother, they killed Luther King," the culprit cried. "Was he stealing shoes when they killed him?" retorted a cop.

Marketing

White reporters moved among the plunderers with impunity. "Take a good look, baby," a looter cried to a carload of newsmen as he emerged from a liquor store on H Street. "In fact, have a bottle"—and he tossed a fifth of high-priced Scotch into the car. Young black girls and mothers, even 7- and 8-year-old children, roamed the streets with shopping carts, stocking up on groceries. "Cohen's is open," chirped one woman to friends as she headed for a sacked dry-goods store with the nonchalance of a matron going marketing. "Take everything you need, baby," Negroes called to each other from shattered store windows. Mingling with the crowds on Pennsylvania Avenue were observers from the German, French, Japanese, Norwegian and other embassies, taking notes to cable home. "It's a revolution," a French Embassy attaché remarked to his companion.

It wasn't. But the sacking of Washington was ugly enough. By midafternoon—with an acrid pall of smoke hanging over the White House and looting going on less than two blocks away—frightened whites and Negro office workers tried desperately to get home, creating a massive traffic jam. Telephone lines were clogged, water pressure was running low and at least 70 fires were blazing. White House aide Joseph Califano set up a special command post to monitor the situation right on the Presidential doorstep. Finally, Lyndon Johnson declared that the Capital was caught up in "conditions of . . . violence and disorder" and as Commander in Chief he first called in some 6,500 Army and National Guard troops, including a contingent stationed on the grounds of the White House itself.

Stability

When looters and pillagers continued to roam the streets, the President ordered in 6,000 more Federal troops. And by late Sat-

*Federal troops patrol the streets in Washington, D.C., during the riots
that followed the assassination of Martin Luther King Jr.*

urday night, the combined forces finally restored some sem-
blance of stability to the Capital.

If the Washington disorders had a bizarre gaiety to them, the
scene in Chicago—where King had led an abortive "End Slums"
campaign in 1966—was bittersweet. Deadly sniper fire crackled
in the South Side slums, and the West Side—the scene of two
major riots since 1965—blazed with more fires than anyone
could count. There was no mistaking the anger of the young
blacks, who watched with solemn satisfaction as whole blocks
went up in flames. "This is the only answer," said one studious-
looking Negro youth as he peered at the flames through gold-
framed spectacles. "It feels good," said another, munching a
vanilla ice-cream cone. "I never felt so good before. When they
bury King, we gonna bury Chicago."

With the tongues of flame dancing against the sky, the talk of
the streets sounded like an invitation to Armageddon. "I thought
I was dead until they killed the King," intoned a 24-year-old gang
leader in a black leather coat. "They killed the King and I came
to life. We gonna die fighting. We all gonna die fighting."

There was little fighting in Chicago. But at least nine Negroes
were killed there, mostly in the act of looting. As elsewhere, the
police who pegged shots at looters were the exceptions to the

rule. And so the plundering went on almost unopposed. Along Kedzie Avenue on the West Side, Negroes carried armfuls and cartloads of booty from ravaged storefronts. "I'm a hard man and I want some revenge," explained one. "King's dead and he ain't ever gonna get what he wanted. But we're alive, man, and we're getting what we want."

Bums

Nearby, a Negro woman begged the vandals to stop. "Come out of that store and leave that stuff," she shouted. "You all nothing but bums. Ain't we got enough trouble with our neighborhood burning down? Where are those people gonna live after you burn them down?" Unhearing—or uncaring—the looters ignored her.

Chicago Mayor Richard Daley had pleaded for peace on TV after King's murder, but his words, too, fell on deaf ears. Finally, with vast areas of the slums in chaos, the National Guard was ordered in. Three thousand guardsmen—many of them black—rolled into the ghetto, with 3,000 more held in reserve. The troops patrolled mostly in four-man Jeeps: a driver armed with a pistol, one man with a carbine and two armed with M-1 rifles. Unlike the green and trigger-happy guard units who performed so ineptly in Detroit and Newark last summer, the Illinois troops were poised enough to handle matters with a minimum of bloodshed. But when the situation heated up again the next day, state officials requested that 5,000 Federal soldiers be deployed to back up the guard. In the end, 12,500 troops were required to bring Chicago back under shaky control.

With disorder sweeping the country, New York, which suffered the nation's first major riot in 1964, braced for trouble. It came soon enough. The immediate post-assassination hours brought a spate of window-breaking and looting to Harlem and in the teeming Bedford-Stuyvesant slum in Brooklyn. Mayor John Lindsay, whose walking tours of the ghettos helped keep the city cool last summer, sped to Harlem to commiserate with the crowds over King's death and defuse the situation. He walked along 125th Street, patting passers-by on the back, then took a bullhorn to speak to the crowds. In a quivering, emotional voice, he began by addressing the Negroes as "Brothers"—a term soul-minded blacks like to use. The mayor barely got in another word. "You got some nerve using that word," one angry youth shouted at Lindsay. Others hurled obscenities at the mayor.

Plea

Next night, Negro youths rode subways to midtown, breaking windows in shops near Central Park and dogtrotting through Times Square. But the police were ready for them, deftly breaking up the roving bands and maintaining order without firing a shot. At the weekend, the mayor was back on the city's slum streets for the third night in a row—and, in the end, he prevailed as an effective force in keeping the racial lid from blowing off in New York. Amidst rising tensions, Lindsay had gone on television to plead for continued calm. "It especially depends on the determination of the young men of this city to respect our laws and the teachings of the martyr, Martin Luther King" and to promise better days ahead. "We can work together again for progress and peace in this city and this nation," he said, "for now I believe we are ready to scale the mountain from which Dr. King saw the promised land."

Perhaps he was right. But the convulsions unleashed by a sniper in Memphis left the nation with ominous questions still to be answered. Were last week's riots a final paroxysm that might purge angry emotions and clear the way for reconciliation? Or were the pictures of the machine gun on the Capitol steps and Chicago in flames only premonitions of an America without Martin Luther King?

A Former Marine Protests the Quagmire of Vietnam

By David Douglas Duncan

In the following selection, photojournalist and retired marine David Douglas Duncan protests the continuing involvement of U.S. troops in the Vietnam War. Duncan deplores a war strategy that turns marines into sacrificial "sitting ducks" while the Vietnamese countryside is constantly bombarded by U.S. air strikes and shelling. Moreover, he questions America's policy of fighting communism by imposing its military might on a peasant nation, arguing that such tactics are damaging the reputation of the United States. Duncan also reveals that American and South Vietnamese soldiers are engaging in torture and other atrocities against the Communist Vietcong and their suspected sympathizers. He concludes that the U.S. bombing of North Vietnam must end and that the United Nations should intervene and mediate an end to the conflict.

I am no kook, hippie, hawk, or dove. I am just a veteran combat photographer and foreign correspondent who cares intensely about my country and the role we are playing—and assigning to ourselves—in the world of today. And I want to

David Douglas Duncan, "One Man Sees the Vietnam War," *Saturday Review*, vol. 51, April 12, 1968, pp. 35–36, 75. Copyright © 1968 by Saturday Review Magazine. Reproduced by permission.

shout a loud protest at what has happened at Khesanh and in all of Vietnam.

I have just returned from Khesanh, where the 26th Marine Regiment is dug in and holding a narrow valley perimeter set between towering, jungle-matted mountain ridges in which an estimated 20,000 to 30,000 North Vietnamese soldiers are easing ever forward toward the Marines' barbed wire, apparently waiting for a propitious moment to launch an all-out human-wave attack. [North Vietnamese] General [Vo Nguyen] Giap has promised to deliver Khesanh as a trophy of war to Hanoi. In Washington, President Lyndon Johnson called together his Joint Chiefs of Staff and demanded that they sign an affidavit stating their convictions that Khesanh would never fall to Giap—which absolves the civilian brass if the military are proved wrong.

Poor Military Strategy

The Marines behind the sandbags at Khesanh were not overjoyed to be designated defenders of the national faith by the President's manifesto-signing political device. They view it as a pistol at their heads and a challenge to Giap to turn Khesanh into another Dienbienphu.[1] They call Khesanh "The Duck Farm"—with themselves sitting targets for Giap's gunners. The Marines' thanks and blessings go out to the transport crewmen who supply them and to the airmen and artillerymen who maintain constant pressure on the enemy through protective air strikes and shelling. Only America can afford this bankruptcy of tactics—defense through deluge. According to the Pentagon, more tonnage of explosives has been dropped around tiny Khesanh than on any other target in the history of aerial warfare—including the atomic bomb that incinerated Hiroshima.

But even if Giap never launches that final attack to breach the wire at the heart of the perimeter, he will have won at Khesanh, in the fullest military sense, by having drawn a reinforced Marine regiment—together with tremendous air and artillery fire—away from General [William] Westmoreland at a time of desperate troop shortages throughout Vietnam, and then having encircled and immobilized it in the most remote corner of the

---

1. Dien Bien Phu, a North Vietnamese city, was the site of a 1954 battle in which occupying French forces were defeated by Communist Vietnamese troops. This battle marked the end of French power in Indochina.

country beyond all reasonable support and supply—to the Marines' frustrated fury.

The "Enemies" Are the Victors

The significance of our frustrations at Khesanh goes beyond discredited military strategy. Judging by evidence from the rest of the world—the non-Communist world—one conclusion is now inescapable: Despite all of the Hanoi oil depots in flames, all of the dropped bridges, every [enemy] MIG-21 [fighter plane] shot down, all of our lost fighter-bomber pilots and those boots of dead paratroopers, and even my heroic, trapped friends at Khesanh, the Vietcong and the North Vietnamese, by just standing up to us and absorbing each body punch we throw, have beaten us in the eyes of the rest of the world—even if every one of their soldiers should die in his sandals, tonight.

We Americans may still be reluctant to admit our defeat at the hands of such an "enemy" for fear of losing "face." Face! For nearly three years we have been conducting all-out war. Anyone who thinks that the employment of the entire military establishment of the United States—involving atomic aircraft carriers, hydrogen bombers, and everything except the ultimate weapon itself—isn't all-out war is a sadly misinformed citizen. Two hundred million Americans trying to crush a peasant nation of 18,000,000 halfway around the earth retain very little "face" in this world.

The war is devouring the long roots of our relationships with those nations who have been our firm allies and friends. It is undermining our economic stability, tarnishing our national character—and sacrificing our youth. And that is why I left the Marines at Khesanh, to protest.

Today, defiant and surly—and self-righteous—America stands nearly alone. Mr. Johnson and Mr. Rusk stubbornly ignore many of us and much of the rest of this deeply concerned world. They are conducting their anti-Communist crusade in our name—with our lives, treasure, and honor. *I protest!*

The Tragedy of Hue

The concept of hanging American prestige and honor and military valor on the defense of Khesanh is sad indeed. Equally tragic was the White House–Saigon method of freeing [the city of] Hue from the North Vietnamese Army and Vietcong political cadres who occupied that most ancient Vietnamese cultural shrine during the first days of the Tet offensive.[2] Prior to Tet, and the disaster it brought upon the entire countryside, Hue was viewed as little more than a tourist attraction for American troops based in Vietnam. The students at its university appeared to sympathize with Ho Chi Minh more than Marshal [Nguyen Cao] Ky, but that was true in many towns.[3] Hue was of no recorded military importance.

Then the Communists captured it and dug in, with their own flag unfurled over the city's historic Citadel. We Americans responded by pounding the Citadel and surrounding city almost to dust with air strikes, napalm runs, artillery, and naval gunfire and the direct cannon fire of tanks and recoilless rifles—a total effort to root out and kill every enemy soldier. The mind reels at the carnage, cost, and almost fanatical ruthlessness of it all. Wouldn't a siege-blockade have been a more effective, and less wasteful, military tactic?

When Kyoto, the religious heart of Japan, was marked for destruction by our Army Air Force during World War II, it was saved at the last moment by Secretary of War [Henry] Stimson. He had visited Kyoto's shrines long before the war, and he held a protective hand over the tiny pinhead marking just another target on a war-room wall map. Assistant Secretary of War John J. McCloy saved classic Rothenberg, Germany, in like manner. As a child in Philadelphia he had fallen in love with an engraving of the romantic medieval town which his mother had brought home from her first trip to Europe. Poor Hue! It had no friends or protectors. Now it is gone.

Various American agencies in Saigon list the ebb and flood of refugees of every battle, totaling them at the end of the year. There is no column in their charts in which to record the opinions or frame of mind of those refugees whose homes went up in smoke during our self-assigned anti-Communist crusade in their country. Nor is there any list, anywhere, recording the number of civilians killed in Vietnam—South Vietnam—since we arrived to protect them from the horror of life under the invader Ho

---

2. Launched on January 30, 1968, the Tet Offensive was a major effort by the North Vietnamese to destroy the South Vietnamese army, force U.S. troops to withdraw, and topple the government in Saigon. Tet was initially successful, but South Vietnamese and U.S. forces eventually recovered and inflicted huge losses on the enemy.   3. Ho Chi Minh was head of the Communist regime in North Vietnam. Marshal Ky was premier of South Vietnam from 1965 to 1967 and vice president from 1967 to 1971.

Chi Minh. No South Vietnamese villager has ever been known to apply a scorched-earth policy by burning his home—yet the ashes of countless houses wash away with each rainstorm.

The War Rhetoric of Vietnam

I protest the tactics. I protest the destruction. And I protest the war rhetoric of Vietnam. Our spokesmen in Saigon explained the Tet offensive this way: By coming out of their holes in everything up to division strength throughout the land to attack various provincial capitals, isolate Saigon, occupy Hue, besiege Khesanh and destroy the rural "pacification" program,[4] the Vietcong and North Vietnamese Army revealed their *weakness:* their all-out assault was nothing but a death gasp born of desperation in the face of our "victories." I, personally, resent being thought so naïve, even downright idiotic. I resent people trying to sell military victories and defeats the same way they pitch 101-millimeter cigarettes, shaving cream, and deodorants.

Another prime example of the Pentagon hucksters' handiwork is that smooth and, surprisingly, widely accepted and printed tag, "free-world forces," used to categorize the "allied" military units deployed in South Vietnam. What they really mean is that approximately one-half million American military men are in South Vietnam—with General Westmoreland reportedly having asked the White House for 200,000 more. In addition, there are roughly 600,000 South Vienamese who are wholly subsidized—and armed—by Washington. Another 48,000 soldiers have come from rebuilt and U.S.-aid-supported South Korea—not exactly a totally independent "free world" nation. Add something like 15,000 Thais, fully equipped with American weapons and sent by a government receiving a massive military dole from the United States; a couple of thousand Filipinos, grateful for the American military aid which helps keep a lately resurgent Huk rebellion in its place, another 8,000 Australians—free of American domination in every sense, yet deeply aware of the white man's precarious role and future in Asia . . . as are the final "free-world forces" from New Zealand, perhaps 1,500 men. Those of us who are a bit older, who spent foxhole time in the heartbreak early months of Korea, remember an era when "allied" meant

4. This was a U.S. military program that aimed to bring humanitarian aid to the Vietnamese people and encourage opposition to Communist Vietcong forces.

sharing risks with military units from Great Britain, France, Ethiopia, Colombia, Turkey, and other battle groups from all over the truly free world.

"Body Count"

Finally, as the worst example of the Vietnam war rhetoric, there is something so fundamentally offensive to Marines everywhere that it is rarely discussed with outsiders. It was forced upon them by the Department of Defense—and they feel it is degrading and humiliating. Their shame—and it should be our national shame—rests on the only two words being used to distinguish between victory and defeat in the war in Vietnam: "body count."

Every "free-world forces" press conference reeks with these two words; each American Armed Forces broadcast is prefaced by the "body count" of that day's action; all records of every skirmish or major campaign feature, above everything else, "body count." It is inescapable, insidious, corrosive—even among veterans of other wars, where victory was represented by hilltops overrun, sea walls breached, then bypassed, islands secured, and cities captured.

Who can remember anyone posting daily "body-count" scores during the battles for Salerno, Iwo Jima, Omaha Beach, Remagen Bridge, Stalingrad, or even Berlin. But, now! Someone, ap-

Soldiers carry a wounded comrade. As the Vietnam death toll increased, many Americans began to doubt continued U.S. involvement.

parently in Washington, decided that there *must* be a way to keep score in a war where there are no victories, ever, in the conventional meaning of the word as related to combat. If "body count" is considered victory, does it mean we threaten genocide to all who oppose us and our arms and our political philosophy?

Sinking into a Quagmire

Admit it—and dislike it—or not, we Americans appear to be sinking into a quagmire of grim impressions being created about ourselves—by ourselves—which may soon cast us in the character of the bullyboys (the neo-Aryan master race) of the coming generation. We seem determined to impose our will and way of life upon most of the rest of the world, whether or not they want it, appreciate it, or ask for it. We justify this dispatch of military and economic missionaries in the name of nation-building and the protection of our vital spheres of interest across the face of the globe, everywhere—especially if anyone can produce even circumstantial evidence that Communists (of any color or breed) might be interested in the place. I protest selling *fear*—of anybody—as America's foreign policy.

Probably few Americans will see a film made for the Bertrand Russell "American War Crime Trials" propaganda extravaganza in Stockholm [in the autumn of 1967]. One would expect to dismiss it as blatant Communist propaganda, too, but it doesn't work quite like that. It runs for seventeen uninterrupted minutes without a soundtrack. The film—black and white—is of rather poor technical quality, which is understandable when one learns it was made from copies of TV films, newsreels, magazine and newspaper photos. Every inch was made by Western, non-Communist newsmen working for our television, magazine, or newspaper services.

The film shows American and South Vietnamese soldiers torturing, beating, mutilating Vietcong and suspected Vietcong prisoners; others, dead, are dragged off triumphantly behind tanks and amtracs. Villages are razed and burned; babies are left dying—also burned; and there isn't a sound from the screen. The film-makers obtained no permission from the Western agencies owning the rights to the original shots—in fact, the pictures were all pirated. So these seventeen minutes will probably never be seen on any commercial American TV or theater screen. But they should be.

Many of us in America, at least men of my generation, can still clearly recall those early terrible newsreels made in Greece and Yugoslavia and Germany itself during the Hitler era. Now, one such newsreel exists which shows American atrocities in Vietnam. Of course, no one has really known—just as surely as many Germans did not know—but I am telling you that the film exists, that the pictures were made by non-Communist newsmen, and that ignorance will be no excuse or defense when the film finally surfaces in this country, as it assuredly will. And there will be no refuge in the argument that our random acts of bestiality were pardonable because enemy atrocities were politically motivated, and even more gruesome.

What Should Be Done

The President of the United States has asked us all, "What would you do if you were here in my place, as President?" Well, Mr. President, I would do three things without delay:

1. I would immediately order the complete cessation of bombing of North Vietnam, *with which we are not at war.* We might still regain a fraction of our lost respect in this world community.

2. I would order all fighter and bomber crews to concentrate on Vietcong and North Vietnamese Army installations and routes of supply in *South* Vietnam until a ceasefire is secured. One might imagine the relief of our pilots at being assigned targets reasonably uncluttered by such operational inconveniences as SAMs [surface-to-air missiles] and antiaircraft fire, and even air-to-air missiles fired by the few surviving MIGs in North Vietnam.

3. I would ask the United Nations to sponsor and police a referendum to be held throughout South Vietnam. The referendum would pose three questions:

   • Do you wish to unite into a single state with North Vietnam?
   • Do you wish to remain a separate and independent state?
   • If you wish to remain a separate and independent state, do you wish the assistance of the Americans in your task of nation-building?

Upon these answers, I would base my future policy and conduct of the war in South Vietnam. I would then concentrate on finding an honorable and stable role for the United States of America in the world of tomorrow.

But there is very little time.

Revolution for the Hell of It: Abbie Hoffman and the Yippies

By Abbie Hoffman

In 1967 left-wing activists Abbie Hoffman and Jerry Rubin founded the Youth International Party, or "Yippies," a group that promoted radical social change through theatrical street protests and satirical confrontations with authority. The Yippies staged a "Festival of Life" during the 1968 Democratic convention in Chicago involving music, speeches, and various antiestablishment actions. In the aftermath of the violence that occurred during the Chicago convention, Hoffman and several other activist leaders were charged with conspiracy to incite a riot, but their convictions were eventually overturned by an appeals court. In the following selection, written several months before the 1968 Democratic convention, Hoffman discusses the revolutionary politics and tactics of the Yippies in his typically irreverent, anarchic style. He also expresses his disdain for the police and their brutal use of force during a Yippie demonstration in New York City.

A mythical interview of questions that are asked and answers that are given. Interviews are always going on. Here's one with myself.

Abbie Hoffman, *The Best of Abbie Hoffman*, edited by Daniel Simon and Abbie Hoffman. New York: Four Walls Eight Windows, 1989. Copyright © 1989 by Abbie Hoffman. Reproduced by permission.

Do you have an ideology?
No. Ideology is a brain disease.
Do you have a movement?
Yes. It's called Dancing.
Isn't that a put-on?
No.
Can you explain that?
Suppose we start the questions again.
OK. Do you have an ideology?
We are for peace, equal rights, and brotherhood.
Now I understand.
I don't. That was a put-on. I don't understand what I said.
I'm getting confused.
Well, let's go on.

For a Free Society

Are you for anything? Do you have a vision of this new society you talk of?
Yes. We are for a free society.
Could you spell that out?
F-R-E-E.
What do you mean free?
You know what that means. America: the land of the free. Free means you don't pay, doesn't it?
Yes, I guess so. Do you mean all the goods and services would be free?
Precisely. That's what the technological revolution would produce if we let it run unchecked. If we stopped trying to control it.
Who controls it?
The profit incentive, I guess. Property hang-ups. One task we have is to separate the concept of productivity from work. Work is money. Work is postponement of pleasure. Work is always done for someone else: the boss, the kids, the guy next door. Work is competition. Work was linked to productivity to serve the Industrial Revolution. We must separate the two. We must abolish work and all the drudgery it represents.
Who will do what we now call dirty work, like picking up the garbage?
Well, there are a lot of possibilities. There won't be any dirty work. If you're involved in a revolution you have a different attitude toward work. It is not separate from your vision. . . . All

work now is dirty work. Lots of people might dig dealing with garbage. Maybe there won't be any garbage. Maybe we'll just let it pile up. Maybe everybody will have a garbage disposal. There are numerous possibilities.

Don't you think competition leads to productivity?

Well, I think it did during the Industrial Revolution but it won't do for the future. Competition also leads to war. Cooperation will be the motivating factor in a free society. I think cooperation is more akin to the human spirit. Competition is grafted on by institutions, by a capitalist economy, by religion, by schools. Every institution I can think of in this country promotes competition.

Are you a communist?

Are you an anti-communist?

Does it matter?

Well, I'm tempted to say Yes if I sense you are. I remember when I was young I would only say I was Jewish if I thought the person asking the question was anti-Semitic.

What do you think of Russia?

Ugh! Same as here. Dull, bureaucratic-sterile-puritanical. Do you remember when [Soviet minister Aleksey] Kosygin came here and met with [Lyndon] Johnson in New Jersey? They looked the same. They think the same. Neither was the wave of the future. Johnson is a communist.

What is the wave of the future?

The [Vietnamese] National Liberation Front, the Cuban Revolution, the young here and around the world.

Doesn't everybody always place great hope in the young?

Yes, I think so. But young people today are very different from previous generations. I think generational revolt has gone on throughout history. Oretga y Gasset in *Man and Crisis* shows that very dramatically. But there are significant differences. The hydrogen bomb, TV, satellites, jet planes—everything is more immediate, more involving. We are the first internationalists. Vietnam rice paddies are as real to me as the Empire State Building. If you don't live in New York, maybe they are more real. We live in a global village. . . .

The Politics of Ecstacy

Do you consider what you are doing politically relevant?

No.

Is that the best answer you can think of?

Well, when you ask a question like that you trigger off umpteen responses in my head. I believe in the politics of ecstasy.

Can you explain that a little more?

No, but I can touch it, I can smell it, I can even dance it. I can even fight it. Politics to me is the way somebody lives his life. Not what they vote for or support or even believe in. I'm more interested in art than politics but, well, see, we are all caught in a word box. I find it difficult to make these kinds of divisions. Northrop, in *Meeting of East and West*, said, "Life is an undifferentiated aesthetic continuum." Let me say that the Vietcong attacking the U.S. Embassy in Saigon is a work of art. I guess I like revolutionary art.

This word game, as you call it. Doesn't that present problems in conveying what you want to say?

Yes, but not in what I want to do. Let me say. . . . Did you ever hear Andy Warhol talk?

Yes, or at least I think it was him.

Well, I would like to combine his style and [Fidel] Castro's. Warhol understands modern media. Castro has the passion for social change. It's not easy. One's a fag and the other is the epitome of virility. If I was forced to make the choice I would choose Castro, but right now in this period of change in the country the styles of the two can be blended. It's not guerrilla warfare but, well, maybe a good term is monkey warfare. If the country becomes more repressive we must become Castros. If it becomes more tolerant we must become Warhols.

Repression and Tolerance

Do you see the country becoming more repressive?

Well, it's very hard to be objective about that. The cops around here are certainly a bunch of bastards. It's winter now and traditionally that's a time of paranoia because it's a time of less action than the summer. Everything has always been geared to the summer. School's out. People in the streets. More action. When you are involved you don't get paranoid. It's when you sit back and try to figure out what's going on, or what you should do. The winter is the hardest time for revolutionists in this country. We probably should hibernate. Everything builds toward the summer. This year it seems more so. Every day we talk of Chicago and the Festival. Every day the news carries a prediction of the "long hot summer." The other day I saw a report from Detroit. People, one white line, one black line, lining up at a gun shop. Meanwhile the mayor is trying to cool things with a nice friendly speech on brotherhood. It was some contrast. Every day has a new report on some new police weapon system. Then there is uncertainty and the tendency to re-examine your tactics. Right now I feel like Dwight Eisenhower on an acid trip. "On the one hand this—on the other hand that." I think it's a case of information overload. See, I am conditioned to perform well in chaos—actual chaos. Say a riot. In a riot I know exactly what to do. I'm not good for the winter. This is my last winter in the North. I have to live in total summer if I am to survive.

Will the summer action bring on more repression?

Oh, I suppose so. I see this country as getting simultaneously more repressive and more tolerant. People run off to Hanoi to collaborate with the enemy. Everybody's smoking pot on the streets. People go on TV and radio shows and spell out in detail plans of sabotage. And simultaneously there is repression. The combination of the two is going to produce highly volatile conditions and that's why many different tactics are needed. Right now revolution is anything you can get away with. It has to be that way because of the nature of the opposition.

What is going to accelerate that process?

Well, Vietnam, the black revolution, and most importantly, WE ARE! All three present this system with more unsolvable problems than it can deal with. You see, there is no solution to the Vietnam war. To leave or to stay is a defeat. No matter what the government does in the ghettos it loses. More aid programs increase the appetite for more demands. More repression produces more anger and defensive violence. The same with the young. I know a girl, Peggy Dobbins, who was a teacher at Brooklyn College. She let the students determine the curriculum; before you knew it, the students wanted to grade themselves. She agreed to go along and of course got the ax from the administration. The more you get, the more you want. The more you are prevented from getting what you want, the more you fight to get it. These are trends that are irreversible, because the government cannot deal with these problems—I mean, the government "deals" with problems rather than solving them.

The Importance of Being Irrelevant

That's pretty political in its analysis. It's New Left in its wording.

Ah, well, it's a regression. I haven't presented any new ideas.

But, well, that's the point. All the ideas are in and have been for some time. I guess I just rap on that from force of habit. I was once in the New Left but I outgrew it. Or perhaps it outgrew me. We differ on many things.

Like what?

Fun. I think fun and leisure are great. I don't like the concept of a movement built on sacrifice, dedication, responsibility, anger, frustration and guilt. All those down things. I would say, Look, you want to have more fun, you want to get laid more, you want to turn on with friends, you want an outlet for your creativity, then get out of school, quit your job. Come on out and help build and defend the society you want. Stop trying to organize everybody but yourself. Begin to live your vision. For example, the other night I was at a benefit for a peace group. Great music, light shows, friends all over the place. It was a good time. Some of the money raised goes to arrange rallies at which speakers give boring political speeches. People think it's a drag but that's the sacrifice to get out the politically relevant statement. The point is, nobody listens to politically relevant statements. In Chicago we'll have a huge free music festival. Everyone already knows our feelings on the issues because we are there. It will have a tremendous impact if we can also project the image that we are having all the fun too. When I say fun, I mean an experience so intense that you actualize your full potential. You become LIFE. LIFE IS FUN. Political irrelevance is more effective than political relevance. . . .

What's the solution? Is there any to the celebrity game?

I don't know. I envision a new life after Chicago. I don't intend to deal with symbolic confrontations. I'm interested in just living with a few friends and building a community. If there is to be confrontation, let it be with the local sheriff rather than LBJ. Maybe this is just a fantasy, though. Maybe it won't happen. I guess everyone dreams of a peaceful life in the country. Especially in the winter.

You're planning to drop out?

Well, dropping out is a continual process. I don't see anything really definite in the future. I just don't want to get boxed-in to playing a predetermined role. Let's say, so much of what we do is theater—in life I just don't want to get caught in a Broadway show that lasts five years, even if it is a success. The celebrity bag is another form of careerism. But you see, celebrity status is very helpful in working with media. It's my problem and I'll deal with it just like any other problem. I'll do the best I can.

Media Manipulation

Is that why the Yippies were created? To manipulate the media?

Exactly. You see, we are faced with this task of getting huge numbers of people to come to Chicago along with hundreds of performers, artists, theater groups, engineers. Essentially, people involved in trying to work out a new society. How do you do this starting from scratch, with no organization, no money, nothing? Well, the answer is that you create a myth. Something that people can play a role in, can relate to. This is especially true of media people. I'll give you an example. A reporter was interviewing us once and he liked what we were doing. He said "I'm going to tell what good ideas you guys really have. I'm going to tell the truth about the Yippies." We said, "That won't help a bit. Lie about us." It doesn't matter as long as he gets Yippie! and Chicago linked together in a magical way. The myth is about LIFE vs. DEATH. That's why we are headed for a powerful clash.

You don't want the truth told?

Well, I don't want to get philosophical but there is really no such animal. Especially when one talks of creating a myth. How can you have a true myth? When newspapers distort a story they become participants in the creation of the myth. We love distortions. Those papers that claim to be accurate, *i.e., The New York Times, Village Voice, Ramparts, The Nation, Commentary*, that whole academic word scene is a total bore. In the end they probably distort things more than the *Daily News. The New York Times* is the American Establishment, not the *Daily News*. The *Daily News* creates a living style. You know: "Pot-smoking, dirty, beatnik, pinko, sex-crazy, Vietnik, so-called Yippies." Compare that to *The New York Times:* "Members of the newly formed Youth International Party (YIP)." *The New York Times* is death. The *Daily News* is the closest thing to TV. Look at its front page, always a big picture. It looks like a TV set. I could go on and on about this. It's a very important point. Distortion is essential to myth-making.

Are you saying that you actually like the Daily News?

Not exactly, but I don't consider it the enemy, in the same way that I don't consider George Wallace the enemy. Corporate liberalism, Robert Kennedy, Xerox, David Susskind, *The New York*

Times, Harvard University—that is where the real power in America lies, and it is the rejection of those institutions and symbols that distinguishes radicals. That is not to say that I love the *Daily News* but that I consider it more honest than *The New York Times*. . . .

Uniforms Are Enemies

How do you feel about cops?

Cops are our enemy. Not each one as a person, naked, say. We're all brothers when we are naked. Did you ever see a fight in a steam bath? But cops in uniform are a different story. Actually, all uniforms are enemies. Just another extension of machine living. The way we dress—in costumes—is in direct opposition to a uniform culture. Costumes are the opposite of uniforms. Since the cops' uniforms also include clubs, handcuffs, guns, etc., they are particularly hated uniforms. I should also add that I've been arrested seventeen times and beaten by police on at least five occasions. I would no more think of asking a cop for help than shooting arsenic to get high.

Who would you ask for help?

My brothers. None of my brothers are cops. You see a cop's principal role is to protect private property. Our goal is the abolition of property. How could I ever call a cop?

Don't they do more than protect property?

Yeah, they kick the shit out of people who have none. Listen. You should have seen Grand Central Station last week during the YIP-IN. Picture this, thousands, maybe ten thousand people, dancing, singing, throwing balloons in the air. Some people decided to climb on top of the information booth; while they were up there they pulled the hands off the clock. This triggered a police riot, with maybe two hundred cops swinging nightsticks charging into people. No warning. No order to clear. About one hundred people were hospitalized, including my wife and me, and over sixty people arrested. There were the police lined up around the clock, guarding it while others smashed skulls. One kid, Ron Shea, tried to come to my rescue while I was being beaten. He was thrown through a glass door and had both hands broken. He may never be able to use one again. Which hands do you think the cops cared more about, the hands on the clock or Ron Shea's hands?

Why did the kids rip the hands off the clock?

I don't know. Maybe they hate time and schedules. Maybe

they thought the clock was ugly. They also decorated the clock with sketches. Maybe they were having fun. When we put on a large celebration the aim is to create a liberated area. People can do whatever they want. They can begin to live the revolution even if only within a confined area. We will learn how to govern ourselves. By the way, this goes on in every revolution. Take Vietnam. In liberated zones the National Liberation Front has schools and theater troupes and hospitals and building programs. The revolutionary experience is far more than just the fighting units.

On Revolution and Death

Do you read revolutionary writings?

Yes, [Che] Guevara, [Regis] Debray, Mao [Tse-tung], [Vo Nguyen] Giap, [Marshall] McLuhan. I find Giap and McLuhan the most interesting. But of course I am totally caught up with Che as a hero. His death moved me far more than, say, that of Martin Luther King. Although King's was a shock also.

What do you think of death?

Well, I must say I have no fear of death. I faced it once about two years ago on an internal level. This is hard to explain. I've actually faced the risk of death a number of times but this one time I actually became paranoid. I was overcome with anxiety. It was unclear what was going on. I overcame that state purely on a mind level and realized that I had the power in me not to become paranoid. It's the paranoia, the living in constant fear of death, that is the real bad trip, not the death itself. I will be surprised if I get a chance to live out my life. Gleefully surprised, but surprised none the less.

Isn't that sort of gloomy?

No! Not really. You can't deny there is a tremendous amount of violence in this country. People who are engaged daily in radical social change are always exposed to that violence. I would rather die fighting for change than surrender. Death in a physical sense is just not seen as the worst of all possible things.

What is?

I don't know. Going to jail. Surrendering. . . . Maybe nothing is really bad, since I am so convinced that we will win the future.

The Rebellion at Columbia University

By Dotson Rader and Craig Anderson

The following selection by *New Republic* writers Dotson Rader and Craig Anderson is a report on the April 1968 takeover of Columbia University by student activists. The students were ostensibly protesting the university's decision to evict people from neighboring buildings in order to expand the campus for a new gymnasium. Along with faculty allies, the students were also purportedly challenging the university's conservative administrative policies and its affiliation with a U.S. defense agency. However, the authors contend, the real purpose of the student takeover was simply to engage in revolution—to take power and help "destroy institutions of the American Establishment." Although the protesters obtained several of their demands, their rebellion culminated in a terrifying raid by local police and a divided, paralyzed educational community.

Sunday night, April 28, Frank Michel stood on the balcony of Mathematics Hall, under a large sign that read, "Rudd Hall, Liberated Zone #5," and looked across the crowded yard toward Low Library, the central administration building, to the lighted windows of the president's office where other protesting students sat in the windows singing and shouting slogans ("Columbia goes from jerk to jerk—Eisenhower to Grayson Kirk"), and yelled to a group of disgruntled jocks below, "We've beaten you bastards! We've won!"

Dotson Rader and Craig Anderson, "Rebellion at Columbia," *New Republic*, vol. 158, May 11, 1968, pp. 9–11. Copyright © 1968 by The New Republic, Inc. Reproduced by permission.

Frank Michel was one of the small group of students, led by Tom Hayden, who had stormed Math Hall on Thursday night and secured it for the liberation. He had been in the building ever since, working with 200 other protesting students, building barricades, pulling up the tiles on the lower floors, greasing stairways, putting plastic bags and vaseline in strategic places to serve as anti-gas protection. He was tired and happy. He was on the committee in charge of feeding over 600 students twice a day in the five liberated buildings. Other committees handled defense and medical details (there was a doctor on duty at all times in each of the buildings). Saturday the Math Building, considered the most radical of the five units, had organized itself into a commune and voted to prohibit drinking, pot, acid and sex.

On the lower campus the black students had opened the doors of Hamilton Hall and stood on the steps outside, behind a protective line of faculty members from the radical caucus of the ad hoc committee. They sang peace songs and greeted students bringing them food and money. They posted a sign renaming Hamilton Hall "Malcolm X Hall" and declared it a part of Harlem. They, too, had won.

Inside the president's office in Low Library students were completing the task of photostating the files of [Columbia University president] Grayson Kirk. They sat on the floor around the desk with huge piles of documents arranged by their political, financial or educational content. Material relating to the IDA [Institute for Defense Analyses] and CIA was the first to be copied. Then private correspondence from the Trustees and from noted political figures (Maxwell Taylor, [Dwight D.] Eisenhower, [J. William] Fulbright, Lyndon Johnson) was photostated.

Gathered around the sundial, the central meeting place on the Columbia campus where protest rallies are traditionally held, over 800 students sat on blankets and huddled around lighted candles and lamps and waited. For they had decided that if the police were ordered against the demonstrators in the buildings that Sunday night they would interpose themselves between the students and the police. Nearby, the ad hoc faculty committee, some 300 professors, argued through the night. They knew that after the crisis the faculty would emerge as the controlling power at the university. The debate now was over the mechanics for exercising that power.

Months before, at an SDS [Students for a Democratic Society] conference in Maryland, the decision had been reached to take physical control of a major American university this spring. Columbia was chosen because of its liberal reputation, its situation in New York and the fact that it was an Ivy League school. SDS felt it was important at this time to disrupt a private, prestige, tactically vulnerable university. Columbia's relations with the West Harlem community, which borders it on two sides, had steadily deteriorated over the years. The decision to begin construction of a gymnasium in Harlem's Morningside Park had united the community against the university. It had evicted hundreds of people from buildings around the university in order to allow for expansion of the campus (and to lower the crime rate in the area).

Columbia was also vulnerable to major disruption because its faculty had become increasingly disenchanted with the leadership of Grayson Kirk and Vice President David Truman, Kirk's chosen successor. Kirk, as spokesman for a conservative Board of Trustees, had steadfastly refused to consider the establishment of a Faculty Senate or to create new constitutional procedures enabling the faculty to exercise power over academic and disciplinary matters. The faculty had already split with the administration over its handling of student protests earlier in the year and over its reluctance to increase the size of Columbia College and to admit to the undergraduate colleges a greater percentage of Negroes.

Originally the two issues to be raised were a general amnesty and a discontinuation of the gym. The amnesty was necessary because SDS had it on reliable authority that its six leaders, on probation for earlier demonstrations, would not be allowed to return to Columbia at the end of this academic year and that the charter of the organization would be revoked during the summer. The gym was made an issue because it would coalesce the black radicals behind the protest.

The question of the university's affiliation with the Institute for Defense Analyses [IDA] was the last to be included in the list of grievances. It was added because the week of April 22 would bring thousands of antiwar protesters to New York and the IDA issue would tie the activities of the radical students on campus to the larger concern of stopping the Vietnam war.

Power Is the Issue

But the three issues were pretexts. The point of the game was power. And in the broadest sense, to the most radical members

of the SDS Steering Committee, Columbia itself was not the issue. It was revolution, and if it could be shown that a great university could literally be taken over in a matter of days by a well
organized group of students then no university was secure.
Everywhere the purpose was to destroy institutions of the American Establishment, in the hope that out of the chaos a better
America would emerge.

With their three issues, SDS were able to bring into their camp
a large following of students concerned with the quality of life
at Columbia and with its relations with the Harlem community.
But after the protest began and the days wore on and the violent
intentions of some of the leadership became evident, more moderate students in the liberated buildings began voting [on] instructions to the Central Committee to moderate both their demands and their tactics. One of the members of the defense
committee in Math Hall, when approached by moderate students
in opposition to his instruction to the commune that it use clubs
and gasoline against the police, retorted, "You fucking liberals
don't understand what the scene's about. It's about power and
disruption. The more blood the better."

Tuesday afternoon, April 23, approximately a hundred radical
students, lead by Mark Rudd, chairman of SDS, had marched to
Morningside Park to protest the building of the gym. They began pulling down the fences that protected the construction site.
The police were called and Rudd led the students away, leaving
the police and the administration with the impression that the
day's protest was over. Instead of dispersing, Rudd directed the
SDS demonstrators in an attack upon Hamilton Hall, a classroom
and administration building of Columbia College. The Acting
Dean of the College, Henry S. Coleman, was trapped in his office and the building sealed. The building was secured by four
o'clock. At four-thirty, Tom Hayden, former national chairman
of SDS and a leader of poverty projects in Newark and Chicago,
arrived at Hamilton Hall as planned. It was Hayden's decision
that produced the withdrawal of white students from Hamilton,
leaving the building in sole possession of the blacks. Mark Rudd
and the Steering Committee opposed Hayden's decision, yet tactically it was one of the most astute decisions the radicals were
to make. It effectively prevented the university from acting
against the seizure of Hamilton Hall. (Rap Brown, Wednesday,
was the first in a chorus of black radicals who would inform the

university that if the police moved against the black students the university would be burned to the ground.)

Faculty Join with the Students

Later that day, with Low Library occupied, the administration attempted to split the radicals by negotiating separately with Hamilton Hall. They offered the blacks total amnesty (something they felt they could not offer generally because the Trustees demanded some of the students be punished), 25 new scholarships specifically for Negro students, and a termination of gym construction. The blacks refused.

Shortly after midnight Thursday the police were called to campus. Vice President David Truman went to the ad hoc committee and informed it the police had been asked to restore order on campus. His announcement was greeted by shouts of "Shame! Shame!" and "Resign!" Evicted by the faculty from the hall the Vice President fled back into Low Library pursued by a score of angry, shouting professors.

One hour later plainclothes police forcibly entered Low Library, using their night sticks to break through the crowd of professors who had blockaded the entrance to the building. Many teachers were hurt. One of the teaching assistants had to be hospitalized at St. Luke's with a head injury. SDS had won a clubbed and outraged faculty to its side.

By early Saturday morning the administration, faced with $11 million in cancelled pledges and hundreds of threatened resignations (among them Eric Bentley's), appeared to capitulate to SDS demands. With the possibility of violence rising hourly, with the growing crowds outside the gates and more and more non-students being spirited on to campus to join the students in the buildings (Dwight MacDonald and Stephen Spender were two of the non-students who joined the protest inside the liberated halls), and with the faculty and student body united in opposition to the administration's use of police force, the president appeared to have little choice. He agreed that the gymnasium would not be built. Within a year he would resign as president for reasons of health and the university would sever its ties with the IDA. An amnesty would be granted in fact if not in name. (The administration was unmoving in its conviction that it could not publicly announce a general amnesty, but Kirk stated to the Steering Committee that no one would receive more than a reprimand.) The Steering Committee agreed not to liberate any more buildings and not to forcibly resist a police raid, if one became necessary. It is on the question of the police raid that the administration and the Steering Committee came to a surprising understanding. It was agreed that one might be necessary if alumni and trustee pressure on the president became so great that he had to protect his own position by affirmative action. SDS, still wanting a public announcement of general amnesty, agreed to allow a bust of the white held buildings if such a statement of amnesty were politically impossible and if, in order to protect its own power over its organization, a bust was necessary to give the appearance that the committee resisted, refusing compromise, to the bitter end. In any case the university would give the Steering Committee sufficient warning to allow students who did not want arrest to leave the buildings in time. No gas would be used.

Until Sunday afternoon the Steering Committee did not inform the liberated buildings of the "no bust" promise. It waited, in part, to keep the threat of a bust as a means of uniting its supporters; also, it was not sure it could trust the president. When it got around to telling the students no bust was coming, it added the words, "at least until Tuesday."

The Bust

Tuesday it came. At 1:30 A.M., when Police Commissioner Leary was assured that Harlem was asleep, 2,000 police, many of them plainclothesmen, 50 mounted horsemen, swept across Columbia, surrounded the liberated buildings, and methodically cleared them one by one. Hamilton Hall was the first to be raided. Police entered without weapons, barehanded, and the blacks meekly followed a lieutenant through the tunnels into a paddy wagon. The president's office was cleared in less than 30 minutes. Police violence was unprovoked and unlimited. A pregnant girl was dragged by the hair down Avery's steps. Professors were beaten senseless. In Mathematics, the students were dragged down six flights of concrete steps, leaving blood so thick the cops were slipping in it. With the halls cleared, plainclothesmen turned on thousands of innocent bystanders on the university lawn. Hundreds were injured. A male student, thrown to the ground, had his eye gouged by a plainclothesman. Horsemen on Broadway rode into terrified crowds, trampling spectators. For two and a half hours, faculty watching through the windows, and wounded students still unremoved from the buildings, witnessed the police destroying furniture, urinating on rugs, dumping files on the floor.

The reaction was swift and emphatic. By that Tuesday afternoon the SDS-called strike had won the majority. The faculty, outraged, moved to increase its power. In direct confrontation with university directives the Committee on Instruction of the college unilaterally ordered classes closed for the week. A Joint Faculties Assembly (prohibited by university regulations) was established, and its executive committee began issuing directives on all university activity.

Frank Michel yelled, "We won!" If polarization and paralysis of a great university is victory, then indeed they did win.

Robert F. Kennedy Is Assassinated

By *Time*

The following account from *Time* magazine details the events surrounding the June 1968 assassination of Democratic senator and presidential hopeful Robert F. Kennedy. After winning the California Democratic primary, Kennedy delivered a victory speech before a crowd of supporters at a Los Angeles hotel. On his way to a post-speech press conference, Kennedy took a back passageway through a hotel kitchen, where he was fatally shot. The suspected assassin, Jordanian immigrant Sirhan Sirhan, was immediately arrested and reported to be an anti-American extremist who objected to Kennedy's support for Israel. As the editors of *Time* report, many Americans speculated that the assassinations of late president John Kennedy, civil rights leader Martin Luther King Jr., and Robert Kennedy were part of a political conspiracy by either the left or the right.

T he circumstances were cruel enough: son of a house already in tragedy's grip, father of ten with the eleventh expected, symbol of the youth and toughness, the wealth and idealism of the nation he sought to lead—this protean figure cut down by a small gun in a small cause. Crueler still, perhaps, was the absence of real surprise.

It was the unspoken expectation of the veteran campaigners who traveled with Robert Francis Kennedy that death was always somewhere out there in the crowd. Occasionally an ordinary cit-

"A Life on the Way to Death," *Time*, June 14, 1968, pp. 16–22. Copyright © 1968 by Time, Inc. Reproduced by permission.

izen, a Negro more often than not, gave voice to the same fear:
They won't let him live. At the first word of the shooting, a reporter with Kennedy workers in San Francisco wrote in his note-
book: "They seemed almost to expect it. There is grief. But more,
there is a kind of weird acceptance. Horrible to see. They've been
through assassinations before.". . .

Faraway Tomorrow

More than anyone else, Robert Kennedy had long felt the possibility that some day people would no longer be able to mention
"the Kennedy assassination" without specifying which one.[1] In
1966, he responded to a question about his long range political
plans by saying: "Six years is so far away, tomorrow is so far away.
I don't even know if I'll be alive in six years." More recently: "If
anyone wants to kill me it won't be difficult." And he was fond of
quoting Edith Hamilton: "Men are not made for safe havens."

Whether gulping fresh air as a tyro mountain climber or rapids
shooter, staring down hostile students in South America or fren-
zied crowds at home, he had only a shrug for death. He made a
point of declining police protection when it was offered—as it
was last week in Los Angeles—and his unofficial bodyguard
went unarmed. To the crowds whose raucous adulation drew him
endlessly to the brink of physician peril, he seemed to offer a
choice: Raise me up with your voices and votes, or trample me
with your strength.

In California, as last week began, it seemed that they had
opted to raise him up. The last day of primary campaigning went
well. While the voters in California and South Dakota were re-
vivifying his candidacy, Kennedy renewed his morale by romp-
ing on the beach at Malibu with [his wife] Ethel and six of their
children. He had to rescue David, 12, from a strong undertow—
but what Kennedy day was complete without a little danger?

Characteristic Mixture

Then it was on to the Ambassador Hotel, near downtown Los
Angeles, to wait out the vote count. Already high spirits rose with
the favorable totals. In South Dakota, he won 50% of the vote, *v.*
30% for a slate favorable to Native Son Hubert Humphrey and

---

1. President John F. Kennedy, Robert's brother, was assassinated in Dallas, Texas, on November
22, 1963.

20% for Eugene McCarthy; then, in the far more crucial California contest, it was 46% for Kennedy, 42% for McCarthy and 12% for an uncommitted delegate group. The two victories gave Kennedy 198 precious delegate votes. Plans were being made for the campaign's next stages in New York and other key states, but first, that night, there were some formalities and fun to attend to: the midnight appearance before loyal campaign workers (and a national television audience) in the hotel's Embassy Room, a quiet chat with reporters, then a large, private celebration at a fashionable nightspot, The Factory.

The winner greeted his supporters with a characteristic mixture of serious talk and cracks about everything from his dog Freckles to his old antagonist, Los Angeles Mayor Sam Yorty. Among Kennedy's last words from the rostrum: "I think we can end the divisions within the United States, the violence."

The next stop was to be the press room. For once, Kennedy did not plunge through the crush to reach the Embassy Room's main door. Bill Barry, his bodyguard, wanted to go that way despite the crowd: he did not like the idea of using a back passageway. Said R.F.K.: "It's all right." So they went directly behind the speaker's platform through a gold curtain toward a serving kitchen that led to the press room. The Senator walked amid a clutch of aides, hotel employees and newsmen, with Ethel a few yards behind. This route took him through a swinging door and into the hot, malodorous, corridorlike chamber that was to be his place of execution.

On his left were stainless-steel warming counters, on his right a large ice-making machine. Taped on one wall was a hand-lettered sign: THE ONCE AND FUTURE KING. At the far end of the ice-making machine stood a man with a gun. Later, a witness was to say that the young man had been there for some time, asking if Senator Kennedy would come that way. It was no trick getting in; there was no serious attempt at security screening by either the hotel or the Kennedy staff.

"I Can Explain"

Kennedy paused to shake hands with a dishwasher, turning slightly to his left as he did so. Before Bobby released the hand of Jesus Perez, the gunman managed to get across the room, prop his right elbow on the serving counter and, from behind two assistant maîtres d'hôtel, fire at his victim just four feet away. Kennedy fell. The hotel men, Karl Eucker and Eddy Minasian, grappled with the assassin, but could not reach his gun hand. Author George Plimpton and Kennedy Aide Jack Gallivan joined the wrestling match. The gun, waving wildly, kept pumping bullets, and found five other human targets. Eight men in all, including Rafer Johnson, an Olympic champion, and Roosevelt Grier, a 300-lb. Los Angeles Rams football lineman, attempted to overpower the slight but lithe assailant.

Johnson finally knocked the pistol out of the stubborn hand. "Why did you do it?" he screamed. "I can explain! Let me explain!" cried the swarthy man, now the captive of the two black athletes and spread-eagled on the counter. Several R.F.K. supporters tried to kill the man with their hands. Johnson and Grier fended them off. Someone had the presence of mind to shout: "Let's not have another Oswald!"[2] Johnson pocketed the gun.

So This Is It

From both ends of the serving kitchen, scores of people pressed in. All order had dissolved with the first shots ("It sounded like dry wood snapping," said Dick Tuck of the Kennedy staff). The sounds of revelry churned into bewilderment, then horror and panic. A priest appeared, thrust a rosary into Kennedy's hands, which closed on it. Someone cried: "He doesn't need a priest, for God's sake, be needs a doctor!" The cleric was shoved aside. A hatless young policeman rushed in carrying a shotgun. "We don't need guns! We need a doctor!"

Television and still photographers fought for position. Assembly Speaker Jesse Unruh swung at one of them. Ethel, shoved back to safety by a hotel employee at the first sound of gunfire, appeared moments later. While trying to get to her husband, she heard a youth scream something about Kennedy. "Don't talk that way about the Senator!" she snapped. "Lady," he replied, "I've been shot." And Ethel knelt to kiss the cheek of Erwin Stroll, 17, a campaign worker who had been wounded in the left shin.

Finally she got to Bobby. She knelt over him, whispering. His lips moved. She rose and tried to wave back the crush, Dick Tuck blew a whistle. The crowd began to give way. Someone clamped

2. John Kennedy's suspected assassin, Lee Harvey Oswald, was fatally shot as he was being transported to a county jail on November 24, 1963.

an ice pack to Kennedy's bleeding head, and someone else made a pillow of a suit jacket. His blue and white striped tie was off, his shirt open, the rosary, clutched to his hairy chest. An aide took off his shoes.

Amid the swirl, the Kennedys appeared calm. *Time* Correspondent Hays Gorey looked at the man he had long observed in constant motion, now prostrate on a damp concrete floor, Wrote Gorey: "The lips were slightly parted, the lower one curled downwards, as it often was. Bobby seemed aware. There was no questioning in his expression. He didn't ask, 'What happened?' They seemed almost to say, 'So this is it.'"

"I Want Him Alive"

The word that Kennedy was wounded had spread back to the ballroom. Amid the screams and the weeping, Brother-in-Law Stephen Smith's controlled voice came through the loudspeaker system, asking that the room be cleared and appealing for a doctor. Within a few minutes, physicians were found and elbowed their way to Kennedy. More policemen arrived; none had been in the hotel, but a police car had been outside on other business. Rafer Johnson and Rosy Grier turned over their prisoner and the gun. The cops hustled the man out, carrying him part of the way past threatening spectators. Jesse Unruh bellowed: "I want him alive! I want him alive!". . .

With Ethel by his side, Kennedy was taken first to nearby Central Receiving Hospital, where doctors could only keep him alive by cardiac massage and an injection of Adrenalin, and alert the better-equipped Good Samaritan Hospital to prepare for delicate brain surgery. As if there were not already enough grim echoes of Dallas and Parkland Hospital, the scene at Central Receiving was degraded by human perversity. A too-eager news photographer tried to barge in and got knocked to the floor by Bill Barry. A guard attempted to keep both a priest and Ethel away from the emergency room, flashed a badge, which Ethel knocked from his hand. The guard struck at her; Tuck and Fred Dutton swept him aside. Then the priest was allowed to administer extreme unction.

At Good Samaritan, meanwhile, a team of neurosurgeons was being assembled. At this stage, there was still some frail hope that Kennedy would live. It was known that he had been hit twice. One of the .22-caliber "long rifle," hollow-nosed slugs had entered the right armpit and worked its way up to the neck; it was relatively harmless. The other had penetrated his skull and passed into the brain, scattering fragments of lead and bone. It was these that the surgeons had to probe for in their 3-hr. 40-min. operation. . . .

Six Counts

As the doctors fought for one life, Police Chief Thomas Reddin worried about another. Dallas, 1963, might not have taught the nation how to preserve its leaders, but it had incontestably demonstrated the need to protect those accused of political murder. The inevitable speculation about conspiracy arose again. There was no support for it, but a dead suspect would certainly become Exhibit A.

The man seized at the Ambassador was taken first to a local police station, then to North Los Angeles Street police headquarters. His arraignment would have to take place at the Hall of Justice, a few blocks away, and Reddin, ever mindful of Dallas, was determined to make it as private a proceeding as possible. First the police considered using an armored car for transporting the prisoner, but decided instead on a patrolman's pickup truck that was, conveniently, rigged as a camper. A judge was recruited to preside at an unannounced 7:30 A.M. session, an hour before the court usually convenes. With Public Defender Richard Buckley representing him, the prisoner was charged with six counts of assault with intent to kill. . . .

Who was the man initially designated "John Doe"? The police had few clues: height, 5 ft. 3 in.; weight, 120 lbs.; eyes, brown; hair, thick, black; accent, foreign, but not readily classifiable. He had a broken index finger and a sprained ankle as a result of the struggle in the pantry, but his basic condition was good. His fingerprints disclosed no criminal record in any law-enforcement agency. Reddin thought he might be a Cuban or a West Indian. He carried no identifying papers, but had four $100 bills, a $5 bill, four singles and some change; a car key; a recent David Lawrence column noting that Kennedy, a dove on Viet Nam, was a strong defender of Israel. . . .

[Soon] the snub-nosed Iver Johnson eight-shot revolver, model 55 SA—a relatively cheap weapon that retails for $31.95—was yielding information. The serial number had been registered with the State Criminal Identification and Investigation Bureau. Within minutes, the bureau's computer system came up with the pistol's original purchaser: Albert L. Hertz of Alhambra. He had bought the gun for protection in August 1965, after the Watts riot. He informed police that he had subsequently given it to his daughter, Mrs. Robert Westlake, then a resident of Pasadena. Mrs. Westlake became uneasy about having a gun in the same house with her small children. She gave it to a Pasadena neighbor, George Erhard, 18. Last December, Erhard sold it to someone named Joe—"a bushy-haired guy who worked in a department store."

With that lead the police quickly found Munir ("Joe") Sirhan, 20, in Nash's Department Store. Joe, said Chief Reddin, was "very cooperative." He and Adel Sirhan, 29, identified the prisoner as their brother, Sirhan Bishara Sirhan, 24, who goes by the nickname Sol. The identification was confirmed by a check of fingerprints taken when Sirhan applied for a state racetrack job in 1965.

All at once, from Washington, Pasadena, Beirut, the Jordanian village of Taiyiba and the loose tongue of [Los Angeles] Mayor [Sam] Yorty, the life and bad times of the accused assassin, Sol Sirhan, came into view. The middle-class Christian Arab family had lived in Jerusalem while Palestine was under British mandate, and the father, Bishara Salameh Sirhan, now 52, was a waterworks employee. The first Arab-Israeli war cost the elder Sirhan his job. Family life was contentious, but young Sirhan Sirhan did well at the Lutheran Evangelical School. (The family was Greek Orthodox, but also associated with other religious groups.)

The family, which had Jordanian nationality, qualified nonetheless for expense-free passage to the U.S. under a limited refugee-admission program sponsored by the United Nations Relief and Welfare Agency and the World Council of Churches. Soon after reaching the U.S. in January 1957, the parents separated. The father returned to Jordan, settled alone in his ancestral village of Taiyiba and became prosperous enough from his olive groves to revisit the U.S. twice. His five sons and their mother Mary all live now in the Los Angeles area. . . .

Mary Sirhan, who has worked in a church nursery for the past nine years, lives with her sons in an old white frame house. The neighbors in the ethnically mixed, lower-middle-class Pasadena neighborhood describe Sol as "nice, thoughtful, helpful." He liked to talk about books and tend the garden; he played Chinese checkers with a couple of elderly neighbors, one of them a Jewish lady. Sol was no swinger, was rarely seen with girls. His brothers told police that Sol liked to hoard his money—perhaps explaining the

$409 he had on him despite his being unemployed recently. He did well enough at John Muir High School to gain admission to Pasadena City College, but he dropped out. He wanted to be a jockey, but could qualify only as a "hot walker," a low-ranking track factotum who cools down horses after the run. Then he got thrown from a horse, suffering head and back injuries.

"Political Act"

Later he worked for a time as a $2-an-hour food-store clerk. His former employer, John Weidner, like several others who know him, remembers his frequently expressed hatred for Israel and his strident Jordanian loyalty. . . .

What had this to do with Robert Kennedy? Journalists quickly recalled that Kennedy, in his campaigning on the West Coast, had restated his position that the U.S. had a firm commitment to Israel's security. In New York, Arab Spokesman M.T. Mehdi talked darkly of the "frustration of many Arabs with American politicians who have sold the Arab people of Palestine to the Zionist Jewish voter." That suggested a motive, but District Attorney Evelle Younger and State Attorney General Thomas Lynch wanted to avoid any such discussion until the trial. Thus they were aghast, and said so, when Mayor Yorty went before a news conference to divulge what he described as the contents of Sirhan's private notebooks, found in the Sirhan home.

According to Yorty, Sirhan wrote that Kennedy must be killed before June 5, the first anniversary of the last Arab-Israeli war, a date that has detonated demonstrations in some Arab countries. Sirhan was also said to have written "Long live Nasser."[3] Yorty went on to characterize Sirhan as pro-Communist and anti-American, and to imply that he might have had some extremist connections. In contrast, the police and prosecutor had been bending over backward to protect Sirhan's legal rights—advising him of his right to counsel and his right to remain silent, calling in a representative of the American Civil Liberties Union to watch out for the suspect's interests.

Aside from its legal implications, Yorty's garrulousness could fuel a new round of conspiracy theories—although conspirators with any skill would hardly have used so light a revolver as a .22. Many found it difficult to believe that the assassinations of John

3. Gamal Abdel Nasser was the president of Egypt.

Kennedy, Martin Luther King and Robert Kennedy were unrelated. Some blamed right-wing extremists; others concluded that all three slayings were part of a Communist plot to divide and weaken the U.S.

For the principals in last week's drama, the speculative and the possible were blotted out by all too real events. Robert Kennedy lived for 25 hours and 27 minutes after being shot on a cruelly elongated Wednesday that the nation is likely to remember in the context of that Friday in 1963. Of all the words last week, some of the most poignant came from Mary Sirhan, who sent a telegram to the Kennedys. "It hurts us very bad what has happened," Mrs. Sirhan said. "And we express our feelings with them and especially with the children and with Mrs. Kennedy and with the mother and the father and I want them to know that I am really crying for them all. And we pray that God will make peace, really peace, in the hearts of people.". . .

Three Widows

Next morning came the news that the family had feared. At 1:44 A.M., Pacific Daylight Time, Bobby Kennedy had died under the eyes of his wife, his brother, his sisters Pat and Jean and his sister-in-law Jackie.

The Los Angeles medical examiner, Dr. Thomas Noguchi, presided over a six-hour autopsy attended not only by members of his own staff but also by three Government doctors summoned from Washington—again a lesson from Dallas. Sirhan was indicted for murder by a grand jury. Meanwhile, once again, the nation watched the grim logistics of carrying the coffin of a Kennedy home in a presidential Boeing 707. This time the craft carried three widows: Ethel, Jackie and Coretta King.

Everywhere, hundreds and thousands watched the cortege firsthand. Millions bore witness by television. The party arrived in New York City at 9 P.M. Thursday, and already the crowd was beginning to form outside St. Patrick's Cathedral on Fifth Avenue. The church was not to be open to the public until 5:30 the next morning, but some waited on the sidewalks through the warm night. Then, thousands upon thousands, in line for as long as seven hours, they marched past the great bronze doors for a glimpse of the closed mahogany casket. The black, the young and the poor were heavily represented: Bobby Kennedy's special constituents.

The Fire Now: Black Power and the Black Panthers

By Eldridge Cleaver

In the following selection, Eldridge Cleaver discusses the development of the black power movement, a radical offshoot of the civil rights movement that advocated self-defense, militancy—and, if necessary, violence—to achieve black liberation in America. Cleaver sees the late Martin Luther King Jr.'s advocacy of nonviolent protest as an outmoded form of resistance that no longer captures the heart of the black masses. Cleaver prefers the legacy of the slain black nationalist leader Malcolm X, whose ideas have laid the groundwork for the Black Panther Party, a revolutionary group that plans to unite black and white radicals in a fight against racism and economic oppression. The author of *Soul on Ice*, Cleaver was a leading spokesman for the Black Panthers. On April 6, 1968, Cleaver was wounded in a gun battle with police, and he was arrested and charged with assault and attempted murder. He wrote this essay in a California jail.

A reassessment of national black leadership has been in order since the [1965] assassination of Malcolm X. The assassination of Martin Luther King [in April 1968] makes such a reassessment inevitable. With the death of King, an entire era of leadership with a distinct style and philosophy, spanning some fifty years, draws to a final and decisive close. A

Eldridge Cleaver, "The Fire Now," *Commonweal*, vol. 88, June 14, 1968, pp. 375–77. Copyright © 1968 by Commonweal Publishing Co., Inc. Reproduced by permission.

new black leadership with its own distinct style and philosophy, which has always been there, waiting in the wings and consciously kept out of the limelight, will now come into its own, to center stage. Nothing can stop this leadership from taking over because it is based on charisma, has the allegiance and support of the black masses, is conscious of its self and its position, and is prepared to shoot its way to power if the need arises.

It is futile and suicidal for white America to greet this new leadership with a political ostrich response. What white America had better do is find out what these leaders want for black people and then set out to discover the quickest possible way to fullfill their demands. The alternative is war, pure and simple, and not just a race war, which in itself would destroy this country, but a guerrilla war which will amount to a second civil war, with thousands of white new-John-Browns fighting on the side of the blacks, plunging America into the depths of its most desperate nightmare, on the way to realizing the American Dream.

Protest as Strategy

When the NAACP [National Association for the Advancement of Colored People] was founded in 1911, it vowed, in its preamble, that until black people were invested with full political, economic and social rights, it would never cease to assail the ears of white America with its protests. Protest as the new posture of blacks toward white America was on its way in, and was destined to dominate the black struggle for the next fifty years. On its way out was the era of begging and supplication, rooted in slavery and the plantation, personified in the genuflecting leadership of Booker T. Washington; chief amongst its myriad treasonous acts was giving black acquiescence to the Southern racist policy of segregation, in Booker T.'s notorious sell-out speech at the Atlantic Exposition in 1896. In the same historic breath, the U.S. Supreme Court made segregation the law of the land when it approved the Separate But Equal doctrine in the case of *Plessy v. Ferguson.*

Dissenting from this confluence of racist ideology, black submission and judicial certification, W.E.B. DuBois led the protest that was institutionalized in the founding of the NAACP; this held sway until 1954, when the U.S. Supreme Court, recognizing that the racist ideology no longer had the necessary allegiance of black leadership, reversed itself and declared Separate But Equal, i.e., segregation, unconstitutional. Black protest leadership, which was born to combat segregation, did not know that when it heard, with universal jubilation throughout its ranks, Chief Justice Earl Warren pronounce the death penalty upon that institution, it was, in fact, listening to its own death knell. There was to be, however, a period of transition between the new out-moded protest leadership and a new prevailing leadership that had not yet defined itself.

Transitional Leadership

The transitional leadership was supplied by Martin Luther King and Malcolm X, and Malcolm X, at his death, had laid the foundation of the new leadership that would succeed both him and King. Martin Luther King was a transitional figure, a curious melange of protest and revolutionary activism. He embodied the first ideological strain in its fullest flower; he contained only a smidgin of the latter. He seemed to be saying to white America: If you don't listen to what I am saying, then you are going to have to deal with what I am doing. As far as the willingness of the white power structure to deal with black leadership goes, Martin Luther King, and the type of leadership he personified, held sway from the launching of the Montgomery Bus Boycott in 1956 down to our own day, when the vestigial remains of leadership from King's transitional era are still frantically trying to cling to power. In reality their leadership is just as dead as that of the lieutenants of Booker T. Washington at the end of their era.

The difference between Martin Luther King and Malcolm X as transitional leaders between the era of protest and our era of revolutionary activism, is that King's leadership was based on the black bourgeoisie and Malcolm's leadership was based on the black masses. In the vernacular of the ghetto, King had House Nigger Power and Malcolm had Field Nigger Power. What we have now entered, then, is an era in which Field Nigger Power and the grievances and goals of the Field Nigger—and the leadership of Field Niggers—will dominate the black movement for justice in America.

Field Niggers, Molotov Cocktails, and Guns

Malcolm X used to tell a little story that points up the difference in perspective and perceived self-interest between the House Nigger and the Field Nigger. The House Nigger was close to the slavemaster. He ate better food, wore better clothes, and didn't have to work as hard as the Field Nigger. He knew that he was better off than his brothers, the Field Niggers, who were kept cooped up in the slave quarters, had only a subsistence diet this side of garbage, and had to work hard "from can't see in the morning until can't see at night." When the slavemaster's house caught on fire, the House Nigger, even more upset and concerned than the slavemaster himself, came running up to say: "Master, master, *our* house is on fire! What shall *we* do?" On the other hand, the Field Nigger, viewing the conflagration from the distance of the slave quarters, hoped for a wind to come along and fan the flames into an all-consuming inferno.

The kernel of truth contained in that story has remained constant from the prison plantations of slavery's South to the prison ghettos of oppression's North, and the urban black, lacking the patience of his forefathers who prayed for a high wind, has opted in favor of the molotov cocktail.

The Black Muslims were the first organization of any significance in our history to understand and harness the volcanic passions of the molotov cocktail–tosser. This organization, which was a transitional organization, rooted in the black masses, based on a protest philosophy with a pinch of revolutionary activism thrown in, made the major contribution of redirecting the dialogue between black leadership and the white power structure, changing it into a dialogue between black leadership and the black masses. This was a necessary by-product of the Muslims' bid to organize black people, because Elijah Muhammad and Malcolm X, in order to get their points across, had to talk over the heads of protest leaders to make themselves heard by the black masses.

Standing toe to toe with the protest leaders, Malcolm and Elijah, talking over their heads, exposed these leaders for what they were, and these leaders, helping to prove the Muslims' point by talking even louder than before, were talking over Malcolm and Elijah's heads—but not to the black masses. They were still chatting with Charlie, a note of desperation having slipped into their tone to be sure. But essentially, what they were saying to Charlie now was that if Charlie didn't listen to them, fund their picayune programs, then he was going to be faced with Malcolm and Elijah. . . .

Black Power

When black leaders stopped chatting with Charlie and started cutting it up with the brothers on the block, a decisive juncture had

been reached, and blacks had seized control of their own destiny.
A full ideological debate ensued. The consensus of this debate
was given to the world on a Mississippi dusty road, when young
Stokely Carmichael leaped from obscure anonymity and shouted,
with a roar of thunder, WE WANT BLACK POWER! How to get it was
the only question as far as the black people were concerned.

There have been a lot of simple answers to this question,
which is by no means a simple one. Black Power, whatever the
form of its implementation, has to solve the question of massive
unemployment and underemployment, massive bad housing,
massive inferior education. It must also deal with the massive
problems of institutionalized white racism manifested in subtle
forms of discrimination that result in blacks being denied equal
access to and use of existing public accommodations and services. From access to medical facilities through the injustices
suffered by blacks in the courts, to the pervasive problem of
racist, repressive police practices, Black Power has to come up
with solutions.

If the experience of other colonized people is relevant, then
the answers given by Huey P. Newton, leader of the Black Panther Party, have to be dealt with. The only real power that black
people in America have, argues Huey, is the power to destroy
America. We must organize this destructive potential, he goes
on, then we can say to the power structure that if black people

*Stokely Carmichael speaks to a crowd at Berkeley, urging African
Americans to fight oppression with "whatever means necessary."*

don't get their political desires and needs satisfied, we will inflict a political consequence upon the system. This is a rejection of the Chamber of Commerce's *laissez faire* myth of the market place that argues to blacks that if they go out and hustle, get themselves educated, learn skills (pull yourself up by your own bootstraps, etc., etc., *ad nauseam*), the American Free Enterprise System will do the rest, that if you don't become President, you are sure at least to make a million bucks. In the age of automation and cybernation, the marketplace has been abolished by the computer. We must make a frontal attack upon the system as a whole, Huey says. We need a redistribution of wealth in America. The form of ownership of the means of production is no longer functional. It is time for the present, non-functional system to be abolished and replaced by a functional, humanistic system that can guarantee a good life for everybody. Everyman is entitled to the best and highest standard of living that the present-day level of technological development is capable of delivering. Every human being is entitled to live. If men must work in order to get the necessities of living, then every man capable of working is entitled to a job. If a man is incapable of working because of a physical inability, then society is responsible for taking care of him for as long as the physical inability exists, for life if necessary. If the businessmen who now control the economic system are incapable of fulfilling the needs of society, then the economic system must be taken out of their hands and rearranged; then the people can appoint administrators to run the economy who can deliver. That is the eternal right of a free people.

The Black Panther Party

The viability of the Black Panther Party's approach to solving problems is testified to by the fact that it has engineered two remarkable feats which constitute the foundation for a revolutionary movement that overlooks nothing, is afraid of nothing and is able to resolve the major contradiction of our time. On the one hand, the Black Panther Party cemented a working coalition with the predominantly white Peace and Freedom Party. On the other hand, it effected a merger with SNCC [the Student Nonviolent Coordinating Committee]. This is the key center of the eye of the storm, because whether they know it or not, whether they like it or not, neither white radicals nor black radicals are going to get very far by themselves, one without the other. In order for a real change to be brought about in America, we have to create machinery that is capable of moving in two different directions at the same time, machinery the two wings of which are capable of communicating with each other. The Black Panther Party, through its coalition with the Peace and Freedom Party and its merger with SNCC, has been the vector of communication between the most important vortexes of black and white radicalism in America. Any black leadership in our era with national ambitions has to embody this functional flexibility without sacrificing its integrity or its rock-bottom allegiance to the black masses.

Stokely Carmichael is Prime Minister of the Black Panther Party. Rap Brown is its Minister of Justice. James Foreman is its Minister of Foreign Affairs, and George Ware is its Field Marshal. At the same time, Huey Newton, Minister of Defense of the Black Panther Party, is running for Congress on the Peace and Freedom Party ticket. The Black Panther Party's nomination for President of the United States, running on the Peace and Freedom Party ticket, is Robert F. Williams, the black leader in exile in the People's Republic of China. Williams picked up the gun against white racism as far back as 1959. If the Black Panther Party succeeds in getting the Peace and Freedom Party to see the wisdom of picking Williams as its Presidential candidate,[1] then a bid for the new national black leadership will begin to come into sharper focus. And America will be astounded by this fact: not only will this leadership bear a charismatic relationship to the black masses, but it also will exercise charismatic leadership upon the white masses as well, and it will reach down into the bowels of this nation, amongst its poor, dispossessed and alienated, and it will set aflame a revolutionary wave of change that will give America a birth of freedom that it has known hitherto only in the dreams of its boldest dreamers. And it will kill, once and for all, all the killers of the dream.

---

1. Eldridge Cleaver was eventually selected for this role.

A New Day for America: Richard M. Nixon's Nomination Speech

By Richard M. Nixon

The following selection is excerpted from the speech Richard M. Nixon delivered when he accepted his nomination for president at the Republican National Convention on August 8, 1968. Noting the year's atmosphere of violence and turmoil, Nixon appeals to those who constitute the "silent majority" of Americans—the decent, law-abiding, hardworking people—claiming that they are the real voice of the nation. Nixon promises to provide leadership for this silent majority by ending the war in Vietnam, by fostering peaceful negotiations with Communist nations, and by restoring respect for law and order in America's cities. He envisions a "new day for America" in which the nation will once again be seen as a symbol of liberty and justice. Nixon served as vice president from 1953 to 1960 and as president from 1969 to 1974. Under the threat of impeachment during the Watergate scandal of the early 1970s, he became the first American president to resign from office.

Richard M. Nixon, nomination acceptance speech before the Republican National Convention, Miami Beach, Florida, August 8, 1968.

Mr. chairman, delegates to this convention, my fellow Americans. Sixteen years ago I stood before this convention to accept your nomination as the running mate of one of the greatest Americans of our time or any time—Dwight D. Eisenhower.

Eight years ago I had the highest honor of accepting your nomination for President of the United States.

Tonight I again proudly accept that nomination for President of the United States.

But I have news for you. This time there's a difference—this time we're going to win. . . .

We're going to win because this great convention has demonstrated to the nation that the Republican party has the leadership, the platform and the purpose that America needs. . . .

We're going to win because at a time that America cries out for the unity that this Administration has destroyed, the Republican party, after a spirited contest for its nomination for President and Vice President, stands united before the nation tonight. . . .

And a party that can unite itself will unite America.

My fellow Americans, most important we're going to win because our cause is right. We make history tonight, not for ourselves but for the ages. The choice we make in 1968 will determine not only the future of America but the future of peace and freedom in the world for the last third of the 20th century, and the question that we answer tonight: can America meet this great challenge?

Let us listen to America to find the answer to that question.

America's Silent Majority

As we look at America, we see cities enveloped in smoke and flame. We hear sirens in the night. We see Americans dying on distant battlefields abroad. We see Americans hating each other; fighting each other; killing each other at home.

And as we see and hear these things, millions of Americans cry out in anguish: Did we come all this way for this? Did American boys die in Normandy and Korea and in Valley Forge for this?

Listen to the answers to those questions.

It is another voice, it is a quiet voice in the tumult of the shouting. It is the voice of the great majority of Americans, the forgotten Americans, the non shouters, the non demonstrators. They're not racists or sick; they're not guilty of the crime that plagues the land; they are black, they are white; they're native born and foreign born; they're young and they're old.

They work in American factories, they run American businesses. They serve in government; they provide most of the soldiers who die to keep it free. They give drive to the spirit of America. They give lift to the American dream. They give steel to the backbone of America.

They're good people. They're decent people; they work and they save and they pay their taxes and they care.

Like Theodore Roosevelt, they know that this country will not be a good place for any of us to live in unless it's a good place for all of us to live in.

And this I say, this I say to you tonight, is the real voice of America. In this year 1968, this is the message it will broadcast to America and to the world.

Let's never forget that despite her faults, America is a great nation. And America is great because her people are great.

With Winston Churchill we say, we have not journeyed all this way, across the centuries, across the oceans, across the mountains, across the prairies because we are made of sugar candy.

America's in trouble today not because her people have failed, but because her leaders have failed. And what America needs are leaders to match the greatness of her people.

And this great group of Americans—the forgotten Americans and others—know that the great question Americans must answer by their votes in November is this: Whether we shall continue for four more years the policies of the last five years.

And this is their answer, and this is my answer to that question: When the strongest nation in the world can be tied down for four years in a war in Vietnam with no end in sight, when the richest nation in the world can't manage its own economy, when the nation with the greatest tradition of the rule of law is plagued by unprecedented lawlessness, when a nation has been known for a century for equality of opportunity is torn by unprecedented racial violence, and when the President of the United States cannot travel abroad or to any major city at home without fear of a hostile demonstration—then it's time for new leadership for the United States of America. . . .

The Vietnam Question

Look at our problems abroad. Do you realize that we face the stark truth that we are worse off in every area of the world tonight than we were when President Eisenhower left office eight years ago? That's the record.

And there is only one answer to such a record of failure, and that is the complete house cleaning of those responsible for the failures and that record.

The answer is the complete reappraisal of America's policies in every section of the world. We shall begin with Vietnam.

We all hope in this room that there's a chance that current negotiations may bring an honorable end to that war. And we will say nothing during this campaign that might destroy that chance.

But if the war is not ended when the people choose in November, the choice will be clear. Here it is: For four years this Administration has had at its disposal the greatest military and economic advantage that one nation has ever had over another in a war in history. For four years America's fighting men have set a record for courage and sacrifice unsurpassed in our history. For four years this Administration has had the support of the loyal opposition for the objective of seeking an honorable end to the struggle.

Never has so much military and economic and diplomatic power been used so ineffectively. And if after all of this time, and all of this sacrifice, and all of this support, there is still no end in sight, then I say the time has come for the American people to turn to new leadership not tied to the mistakes and policies of the past. That is what we offer to America.

And I pledge to you tonight that the first priority foreign policy objective of our next Administration will be to bring an honorable end to the war in Vietnam.

We shall not stop there. We need a policy to prevent more Vietnams. All of America's peace-keeping institutions and all of America's foreign commitments must be reappraised.

Over the past 25 years, America has provided more than $150-billion in foreign aid to nations abroad. In Korea, and now again in Vietnam, the United States furnished most of the money, most of the arms, most of the men to help the people of those countries defend themselves against aggression. Now we're a rich country, we're a strong nation, we're a populous nation but there are 200 million Americans and there are two billion people that live in the free world, and I say the time has come for other nations in the free world to bear their fair share of the burden of defending peace and freedom around this world.

What I call for is not a new isolationism. It is a new internationalism in which America enlists its allies and its friends around the world in those struggles in which their interest is as great as ours.

An Era of Negotiations

And now to the leaders of the Communist world we say, after an era of confrontations, the time has come for an era of negotiations.

Where the world super-powers are concerned there is no acceptable alternative to peaceful negotiation. Because this will be a period of negotiations we shall restore the strength of America so that we shall always negotiate from strength and never from weakness.

And as we seek through negotiations let our goals be made clear. We do not seek domination over any other country. We believe deeply in our ideas but we believe they should travel on their own power and not on the power of our arms. We shall never be belligerent. But we shall be as firm in defending our system as they are in expanding theirs.

We believe this should be an era of peaceful competition not only in the productivity of our factories but in the quality of our ideas. We extend the hand of friendship to all people. To the Russian people. To the Chinese people. To all people in the world. And we shall work toward the goal of an open world, open sky, open cities, open hearts, open minds. . . .

Restoring Respect for America

My friends, America is a great nation. It is time we started to act like a great nation around the world.

It's ironic to note, when we were a small nation, weak militarily and poor economically, America was respected. And the reason was that America stood for something more powerful than military strength or economic wealth.

The American Revolution was a shining example of freedom in action which caught the imagination of the world, and today, too often, America is an example to be avoided and not followed.

A nation that can't keep the peace at home won't be trusted to keep the peace abroad. A President who isn't treated with respect at home will not be treated with respect abroad. A nation which can't manage its own economy can't tell others how to manage theirs.

If we are to restore prestige and respect for America abroad, the place to begin is at home—in the United States of America. . . .

So let us have order in America, not the order that suppresses dissent and discourages change but the order which guarantees the right to dissent and provides the basis for peaceful change. . . .

Let those who have the responsibility to enforce our laws, and our judges who have the responsibility to interpret them, be dedicated to the great principles of civil rights. But let them also recognize that the first civil right of every American is to be free from domestic violence. And that right must be guaranteed in this country.

And if we are to restore order and respect for law in this country, there's one place we're going to begin: We're going to have a new Attorney General of the United States of America.

I pledge to you that our new Attorney General will be directed by the President of the United States to launch a war against organized crime in this country.

I pledge to you that the new Attorney General of the United States will be an active belligerent against the loan sharks and the numbers racketeers that rob the urban poor in our cities.

I pledge to you that the new Attorney General will open a new front against the pill peddlers and the narcotics peddlers who are corrupting the lives of the children of this country.

Because, my friends, let this message come through clear from what I say tonight. Time is running out for the merchants of crime and corruption in American society. The wave of crime is not going to be the wave of the future in the United States of America.

We shall re-establish freedom from fear in America so that America can take the lead of re-establishing freedom from fear in the world.

And to those who say that law and order is the code word for racism, here is a reply: Our goal is justice—justice for every American. If we are to have respect for law in America, we must have laws that deserve respect. Just as we cannot have progress without order, we cannot have order without progress.

And so as we commit to order tonight, let us commit to progress. . . .

The American Generation

My fellow Americans, I believe that historians will recall that 1968 marked the beginning of the American generation in world

Richard Nixon greets attendees at a GOP conference in Washington, D.C. He accepted the nomination for the presidency in 1968.

history. Just to be alive in America, just to be alive at this time is an experience unparalled in history. Here's where the action is.

Think: Thirty-two years from now most of the Americans living today will celebrate a New Year that comes once in a thousand years.

Eight years from now, in the second term of the next President, we will celebrate the 200th anniversary of the American Revolution.

And by our decision in this we—all of us here, all of you listening on television and radio—we will determine what kind of nation America will be on its 200th birthday. We will determine what kind of a world America will live in in the year 2000.

This is the kind of a day I see for America on that glorious Fourth eight years from now: I see a day when Americans are once again proud of their flag; when once again at home and abroad it is honored as the world's greatest symbol of liberty and justice.

I see a day when the President of the United States is respected and his office is honored because it is worthy of respect and worthy of honor. I see a day when every child in this land, regardless of his background, has a chance for the best education that our wisdom and schools can provide, and an equal chance to go just as high as his talents will take him.

I see a day when life in rural America attracts people to the country rather than driving them away.

I see a day when we can look back on massive breakthroughs in solving the problems of shims and pollution and traffic which are choking our cities to death.

I see a day when our senior citizens and millions of others can plan for the future with the assurance that their government is not going to rob them of their savings by destroying the value of their dollar.

I see a day when we will again have freedom from fear in America and freedom from fear in the world. I see a day when our nation is at peace and the world is at peace and everyone on earth—those who hope, those who aspire, those who crave liberty will look to America as the shining example of hopes realized and dreams achieved.

The Need for Total Commitment

My fellow Americans, this is the cause I ask you to vote for. This is the cause I ask you to work for. This is the cause I ask you to commit to not just for victory in November but beyond that to a new Administration because the time when one man or a few leaders could save America is gone. We need tonight nothing less than the total commitment and the total mobilization of the American people if we are to succeed.

Government can pass laws but respect for law can come only from people who take the law into their hearts and their minds and not into their hands.

Government can provide opportunity, but opportunity means nothing unless people are prepared to seize it.

A President can ask for reconciliation in the racial conflict that divides Americans, but reconciliation comes only from the hearts of people.

And tonight, therefore, as we make this commitment, let us look into our hearts, and let us look down into the faces of our children.

Is there anything in the world that should stand in their way? None of the old hatreds mean anything when you look down into the faces of our children. In their faces is our hope, our love and our courage.

Tonight, I see the face of a child. He lives in a great city, he's black or he's white, he's Mexican, Italian, Polish, none of that matters. What matters he's an American child.

That child in that great city is more important than any politician's promise. He is America, he is a poet, he is a scientist, he's a great teacher, he's a proud craftsman, he's everything we've ever hoped to be in everything we dare to dream about.

He sleeps the sleep of a child, and he dreams the dreams of a child. And yet when he awakens, he awakens to a living nightmare of poverty, neglect and despair.

He fails in school, he ends up on welfare. For him the American system is one that feeds his stomach and starves his soul. It breaks his heart. And in the end it may take his life on some distant battlefield.

To millions of children in this rich land this is their prospect, but this is only part of what I see in America.

I see another child tonight. He hears a train go by. At night he dreams of faraway places where he'd like to go. It seems like an impossible dream. But he is helped on his journey through life. A father who had to go to work before he finished the sixth grade sacrificed everything he had so that his sons could go to college.

A gentle Quaker mother with a passionate concern for peace, quietly wept when he went to war but she understood why he had to go.

A great teacher, a remarkable football coach, an inspirational minister encouraged him on his way. A courageous wife and loyal children stood by him in victory and also in defeat.

And in his chosen profession of politics, first there were scores, then hundreds, then thousands, and finally millions who worked for his success.

And tonight he stands before you, nominated for President of the United States of America.

A New Dawn

You can see why I believe so deeply in the American dream.

For most of us the American revolution has been won, the American dream has come true. What I ask of you tonight is to help me make that dream come true for millions to whom it's an impossible dream today. . . .

My fellow Americans, the dark long night for America is about to end.

The time has come for us to leave the valley of despair and climb the mountain so that we may see the glory of the dawn, a new day for America, a new dawn for peace and freedom to the world.

The Chicago Riots Mar the 1968 Democratic Convention

By Gale Research

On August 25, 1968, the Democratic Party opened its national convention in Chicago, Illinois. Several organizations and counterculture groups staged antiwar demonstrations and parades during the days of the convention. Police and National Guard troops responded to the protesters with force, resulting in hundreds of injuries and arrests. The height of the melee was televised just as Hubert Humphrey received the Democratic presidential nomination. As a result of the riots, Humphrey's standing in the polls fell, and he was narrowly defeated by Richard Nixon in the 1968 election.

B y all measures, 1968 was one of the most tumultuous years in twentieth century American political history. The Vietnam War increased in intensity, escalating American casualties and citizen disillusionment with the conflict. Racial tensions exploded into riots in many cities, particularly after the assassination of Martin Luther King, Jr. Demonstrations on college campuses against the war brought students into conflict with police who were often called to maintain order. Lyndon B. John-

Gale Research, "Chicago Riots Mar the Democratic Convention, August 24, 1968–August 30, 1968," *DISCovering U.S. History.* Farmington Hills, MI: Gale Research, 1997. Copyright © 1997 by Gale Group. Reproduced by permission.

son, who had been elected president with one of the largest pluralities in history four years earlier, responded to the turmoil by deciding not to run for a subsequent term in office.

Frustrations with the political process mounted on both the Left and the Right. Left-wing thinkers attributed problems to the underlying causes of the demonstrations, notably the continuing war in Vietnam and the government's failure to address racial and social inequities quickly enough. These individuals often argued for radical change in the political, judicial, and executive systems. Right-wing politicians argued that the demonstrators themselves were the problem and blamed the confrontations on indulgent political officials who failed to use sufficient force to suppress protests. George Wallace ran for the presidency as an Independent candidate, demanding "law and order"—a catchphrase that became synonymous with the repression of political dissent.

Most American citizens fell somewhere between these two extremes. There was a growing feeling that the government's Vietnam policy was not working and that many social injustices went unaddressed. Most citizens also feared the increased polarization of the society and hoped that the conflicts would be worked out within the confines of the present political system. Many young people who opposed the war expressed this hope by working on Eugene McCarthy's or Robert Kennedy's campaigns for the Democratic presidential nomination. Both candidates enjoyed success in the Democratic primaries by taking a stance against Johnson's war policies; Eugene McCarthy continued this crusade after Robert Kennedy's assassination. Many McCarthy delegates perceived the Democratic National Convention as a forum for challenging the administration's Vietnam policy and its candidate, Vice President Hubert H. Humphrey. The Democratic National Convention, for several reasons, proved a suitable place for the conflict between left- and right-wing extremists to boil over into violent confrontations.

Contributing Factors

First, the city [of Chicago] was run by Mayor Richard Daley, an old-style political boss who controlled the state Democratic Party system with unchallenged authority. Daley viewed disruptive demonstrations and calls for more participation in the choice of presidential candidates as a direct affront. He made this position clear during disturbances following the death of Martin Luther

King, Jr., and during a peace march in Chicago in April, 1968. When police acted with restraint in the first case, they were chastised by Daley, who had issued a command to "shoot to kill arsonists and shoot to maim looters." When police attacked demonstrators, bystanders, and media personnel in the second case, the mayor's office ignored the violence.

Second, several groups planned to organize demonstrations against the war and called upon supporters to join them in Chicago for the convention. Four of the main groups were the National Mobilization to End the War in Vietnam, led by David Dellinger and Rennie Davis; the Yippies, led by Jerry Rubin and Abbie Hoffman, who attempted to combine the counterculture life-style of the hippies with a political statement against the war; Students for a Democratic Society (SDS), a campus antiwar group led by Tom Hayden; and the Coalition for an Open Convention, led by Martin Slate, which attempted to bring together antiwar and anti-Humphrey forces in the Democratic Party. Some McCarthy supporters also came to Chicago, despite the senator's warning to stay away. The first four groups officially intended to demonstrate and rally but avoid disrupting the convention. Rumors and careless statements by some group leaders, and the presence of more militant minor groups, undermined these peaceful intentions. All four groups applied unsuccessfully for permits for marches, rallies, and access to the public parks for sleeping. The seemingly inevitable public assemblies were therefore illegal from the start, increasing the potential for confrontation.

Finally, the Chicago convention became a symbolic forum for the conflict between "old" and "new" politics. For many demonstrators, Humphrey's presidential candidacy represented a continuation of the back-room politics which ignored public dissent on Vietnam and other issues. They viewed the convention as a confrontation between traditional machine politics, represented by Daley and the Democratic Party's old guard, and the new (and often idealized) politics of increased citizen participation, represented by McCarthy supporters and young protest leaders.

Violent Clashes

As expected, the city's prohibition of demonstrations was only partially successful in stopping protesters from arriving in Chicago. Group leaders' early estimates of the number of participants proved to be overly optimistic, but approximately five thousand protesters had gathered in Lincoln Park by the Sunday evening before the convention was to begin. The first confrontations between demonstrators and law enforcement officials occurred following a peaceful afternoon march. The police, enforcing a ban on overnight camping in the park, randomly attacked protesters, bystanders, and media personnel, chasing them into the city's Old Town district.

This pattern was repeated on August 28, following a legal rally in Grant Park, across from the Hilton Hotel where a number of delegates were staying. The rally was attended by SDS, Yippie, National Mobilization, and Open Convention protesters in addition to a number of older, nonviolent demonstrators, including disillusioned McCarthy supporters. Altercations began at a flagpole, where an American flag was lowered. Police attacked Rennie Davis when he attempted to restore order by assembling rally marshals between the protesters and the police. The rally concluded and the demonstrators marched out with unclear objectives, eventually joining a legal march by the Southern Christian Leadership Conference (SCLC). Approximately seven thousand people eventually massed in front of the Hilton, where television cameras were present. Police allowed the SCLC marchers to pass but began clearing other protesters from the site.

Suddenly, several police stormed the crowd and began indiscriminately attacking protesters and innocent bystanders with clubs, mace, and fists. A few protesters fought back with rocks and other projectiles. The violence continued for about three hours in front of the hotels occupied by Hubert Humphrey, George McGovern, and Eugene McCarthy. Television cameras recorded the entire confrontation despite police attacks on media personnel. The antiwar protesters retreated back to Grant Park for an all-night rally just as Humphrey received the Democratic nomination for president. Humphrey's victory was to be remembered for the clashes between police and demonstrators which were televised as the final convention votes were tallied.

The Impact of the Event

The immediate impact of the events in Chicago were felt within an already divided Democratic Party. There was an upsurge of support for the "law and order" stances of George Wallace and, in a milder version, Richard Nixon. Humphrey's standing in the polls suffered accordingly, even though he regained most of his support and lost the November election to Nixon by only .7 percent of the vote.

Longer-term effects involved the way in which the public regarded the press and its role in covering political upheavals. The Federal Communications Commission answered many complaints about the media's coverage of the violence. The National Commission on the Causes and Prevention of Violence held public hearings in late 1968 to evaluate whether the press contributed to such confrontations in Chicago and other cities. The press was cleared of complicity, but arguments about the impact of mass media on protest activity were to continue for years to come.

Also charged with complicity in the Chicago violence were Rennie Davis, Tom Hayden, David Dellinger, Bobby Seale, Abbie Hoffman, Jerry Rubin, and Mobilization officials Lee Weiner and John Froines. These individuals became known as the Chicago Seven after Seale was removed from the courtroom and tried separately. All were charged with conspiracy to riot by Attorney General John Mitchell, even though most had never even met one another until the convention. By this action, Nixon signaled his intolerance of protests and demonstrations. He made attacks on protesters one cornerstone of his 1972 presidential campaign, adapting George Wallace's hard-line "law and order" stance to a more moderate audience.

Perhaps the farthest reaching effects of the Chicago demonstrations, however, were the changes they prompted in the procedures for choosing presidential candidates. The unrest was interpreted as one sign that the back-room selection of candidates for office needed to be opened up to wider citizen participation. By 1972, the rules governing selection had been changed dramatically, providing for an expanded primary system and a selection process for delegates to the Democratic convention including significant numbers of women, young people, and racial minorities. In a final ironic footnote, the Daley delegation to the 1972 convention failed to meet the national party quotas for women and minorities and was not seated.

The changes in the presidential selection process, cannot, of course, be traced solely to the events in Chicago in 1968. The clashes, however, remained a major symbol of the conflict between the old and new politics, a conflict which redefined the direction and agenda of American politics for the following two decades.

The Life and Death of the Hippies

By William W. MacDonald

The hippies—the rebellious, long-haired youths who reject middle-class materialism and conventional values—have captured America's attention, writes William W. MacDonald in the following essay. While they are often perceived as drug-taking drop-outs who protest against the Vietnam War, true hippies actually object to political activism, preferring to effect change by setting an example through their alternative lifestyle. This lifestyle includes indulgence in hallucinogens, an ethic of communal love, and experimentation with mysticism and Eastern religions. The hippie movement is in the process of dying, the author notes, because it is prone to escapism and self-indulgence and has no sustaining ideology or discipline. However, the hippies' criticism of society's greed and hypocrisy could be beneficial for America, he concludes. MacDonald was a history professor at Lamar State College in Beaumont, Texas, when he wrote this essay.

No generation, it is said, can predict the weapons that the next one will use against it. But surely few Americans who grew up during the Depression and struggled to win middle-class privileges and profits for their families would have dreamed that by 1968 some of their most gifted sons and daughters would purposely be hurrying from riches to rags. Today, these visible, audible and sometimes remarkable young rebels, loosely called hippies, have stopped cutting their hair, dis-

William W. MacDonald, "Life and Death of the Hippies," *America*, vol. 119, September 7, 1968, pp. 150–55. Copyright © 1968 by America Press, Inc., 106 West 56th Street, New York, NY 10019, www.americamagazine.org. All rights reserved. Reproduced by permission.

carded Ivy League suits and walked out of their parents' subur-
ban homes to walk barefoot through the streets, strum guitars and
tell us all to make love instead of war.

Though there are mods in England and provos in Denmark,
hippies are essentially an American phenomenon. Because of several hundred articles, numerous books and dozens of television
documentaries, hippieland encompasses every major U.S. city. It
has a population of about 250,000. So pervasive has been the
world of hippiedom that even [the Russian newspaper] *Pravda*
was moved to praise the hippies' social revolutionary efforts. So
infectious is hippieness that it prompted a member of the Atlanta
Chamber of Commerce to state, after some Georgians complained
about a 100-member hippie community: "If psychedelic education is the trend, then goddam it, let's have it here!"

The hippies and their movement are, of course, an "in" movement, and they are making money for the hated Establishment.
The hippies have found their forms and ideas exploited in fashions, music, art, advertising and cheap novelties. During the past
year there was a play in New York called *The Freaking Out of
Stephanie Blake*, and a movie called *The Love-Ins*. In San Francisco there is a clip joint offering a "Topless Hippie Sex Orgy."
In Haight-Ashbury one can consume a "loveburger," and in
Boston there is a rock and roll station that calls itself the "Station of Flower Power." The hippie reaction to all this is contempt
and frustration.

Problems Facing the Hippie Movement

This is probably a unique time to speak of the hippie cult, for
most observers, both hippie and non-hippie, are predicting its
sudden death. John J. O'Connell, editor of *This Week* magazine,
was the first to speak of "post-hippie days," but the influential
New York Times Magazine, which only last October presented
June Bingham as tutor to teach us hippie vocabulary, has begun
to nail down the coffin lid with an article titled "Love is Dead."
Time gleefully buried the movement under tons of split infini-
tives, innuendoes and distortions. *Life* and *Look* have run several
stories explaining how conventional middle-class parents are
hunting down their unconventional runaway children throughout
hippieland after the brutal murder of two young hippies a couple
of months ago. And *Newsweek* recently had a long article, "Trouble in Hippieland."

Most observers find that there are three fundamental problems facing the hippie movement. The first is the failure of the love ethic or flower power to convert its antagonists. Commenting on the problems of the flower children in the cities, a 19 year old hippie said: "It's showed us something, man. It's showed us you can't find God and love in Sodom and Gomorrah. So it's time to split." Another remarks: "I know it sounds crazy, but how can you talk love to middle-aged creeps who hate you?" In brief, one of the major problems facing the hippies is miscalculation: the urban slum is not a suitable setting for Eden's love and beauty.

The second problem facing the hippies is the war that politicians, policemen and minority groups have declared against all hippies. The hippie communities of San Francisco, New York and Boston are now under siege. In Cambridge, Mass., the mayor has launched total war on what he calls the "hipbos" (the suffix stands for body odor). He finds them a threat to common decency; he believes they are mentally deranged, and he is working to effect their destruction.

The police have always been a threat to nonconforming minority groups, and in some places the hippies have become their visible public enemy number one. To the police, the hippies represent runaway kids, vagrancy, drugs, pornographic books, hazardous housing, garbage. To the hippies, the police represent false arrest, illegal arrest, incitement to arrest, swinging clubs, obscene men diseased with blind hatred. From the hippie side, no cop ever becomes a cop through a sense of justice or decency or humanitarianism. The cop is *their* visible enemy number one, the living symbol of all the vice and hypocrisy of the Establishment.

The minority groups—Puerto Ricans, Mexicans, Jews, Italians, etc.—also view the hippies with distaste and often with downright hostility. It is difficult enough to understand love, let alone practice it in a world of urban hatred between peoples. "The hippies really bug us," one young Negro explained to a reporter, "because they can come down here and play their games for a while and escape." "After the hippies go back to their middle-class homes," declared another Negro observer, "we'll still be here." Another Negro in Haight-Ashbury satirically indicted the hippie movement in this way: "The hippies have turned a nice neighborhood into a slum. If some hippies moved next door to me I would move out, because I couldn't tolerate the filth."

In fact, the hippies are not really on the Negroes' side, for they interpret the Negroes' demand for a better life as crassly materialistic and hopelessly middle-class. "Civil rights is a game for squares," one hippie informed Jack Newfield, as he wrote in the *Nation*. "Why should I demonstrate to get the spades all the things I am rejecting?" Newfield concludes that the hippies have a romantic attachment to the Negro as an Outsider, but as soon as he becomes an accepted member of the social order, they view him as part of the hated Establishment.

The Pseudo-Hippie

The final problem facing the hippies is the non-hippie hippie, the pseudo-hippie. These are usually called "plastic" hippies; they are weekend hippies who have regular Establishment jobs during the week and practice the hippie bit on the weekend. These plastic hippies dominate the movement; they are pleasure seekers out for kicks; they are image hippies, media hippies. The trouble is that they indulge in the hippie actions but totally ignore the hippie message. Henry Brandon, writing in the *Saturday Review*, tells us that the "true" hippies, "who were in revolt against the greed of a materialistic society, who resent the abuses of affluence, are suddenly disenchanted by the failure of their own hippie society, which more and more are joining just for kicks."

Last October the *Berkeley Barb*, an underground newspaper, proclaimed the "Death of Hip," because the news media's image of hippieism enticed many dissatisfied young people to Haight-Ashbury—people who had not made an internal commitment to drop out. Instead of "doing their thing," these people were becoming "media image hippies." The *Barb* then proclaimed a "Declaration of Independence" for the "Rebirth of Free Men," and asked everyone to give up their image hippie clothes, beads, beards and earrings, for this would separate the image hippies from the true hippies, the uncommitted hippies from the committed hippies, and a new movement of "Freebies" would begin.

To the average person, hippies are still those who wear beards and sandals, drop out of school, smoke pot and take LSD, burn their draft cards and demonstrate against the war in Vietnam. This familiar and stereotyped picture, however, is inaccurate. There are really two basic groups of protesters and dissenters in the United States today, the hippies and the New Left. Both these groups share common hatreds. They hate with a passion the Establishment, racial prejudice, American culture, traditions and values, and American foreign policy. They hate with fluctuating intensity President [Lyndon] Johnson, Hubert Humphrey, Robert Kennedy, Ronald Reagan and Shirley Temple. . . .

What unites the New Left and the hippies is their hatred; what separates them is their philosophy on how to eradicate the cancers in American society. The New Left is a conglomerate group of people who sponsor and seek revolutionary action, with emphasis on the action. It embraces groups like the Students for a Democratic Society, the Dubois Clubs, the Progressive Labor Party, the Convention for a New Politics, and a number of Black Power groups. It is composed of people like Staughton Lynd, Tom Hayden, Robert Scheer and John Gerassi. The New Left's goal is participatory democracy, the right of people actually to endorse decisions that affect them. Its actions and platform are most certainly revolutionary, sometimes violent and perhaps even subversive. . . .

A Rejection of Dissent

The hippies, however, though revolutionary, are neither subversive nor violent. They are, in fact, totally opposed to action; they are completely apathetic to political problems. While the hippies reject the capitalist emphasis on "mine"—whether my house, my money, my gadgets, my child, or my art—they also reject the acquisitive and violent ideology of the Communists and the New Left. The hippies oppose dissent because they find dissent meaningless, absurd and stupid. They hope to change America by example. . . .

The hippies feel that the kinds of changes that need to be made in America cannot be made through political action, cannot be made by electing Presidents or Senators or Congressmen. Short of killing people, which they oppose, the changes can be made, they say, only by changing people's attitudes and values, by changing the heads of men, by convincing people to give up peacefully the "hang-up" delusions that inhibit accurate perception and prevent appropriate responses. And the hippies are quite openly, defiantly and consistently going about doing just that.

Middle-Class Dropouts

To most Americans the alarming and most maddening aspect of the entire movement is that the hippies are middle-class American children to the bone. They aren't Negroes disaffected by color; they aren't poverty-stricken kids thumbing their noses at an affluent America. They are boys and girls with white skins from the right side of the economy, and they come from all-American cities all the way from Bangor, Me., to San Francisco.

The hippies are not an isolated band of juvenile misfits. If they are a lunatic fringe, they are the fringe of a largely invisible movement a hundred times the size of their own very visible cult. This movement has grown up on every college campus in the country and has opened a gap between the generations wider than any that Scott Fitzgerald ever thought of. Richard Flack, a psychiatrist writing in *Psychology Today*, has studied today's rebellious youth and found that they are attracted to the hippie cult not because they are economically deprived or because their opportunities for mobility, or for anything else, are blocked. The hippies are usually highly advantaged kids who are indifferent to, or repelled by, the best opportunities for high status and income. Most hippies, Flack argues, are recruited from a very special kind of middle and upper-middle class family. In most of these families the parents are highly educated, extraordinarily well-off, permissive and democratic. The hippies, he concludes, are rebelling not against strict, oppressive, conservative or religiously oriented parents, but against the exact opposite, liberal parents.

Hippies insist on historical discontinuity. They believe both in the infinite plasticity of human nature and also in themselves as a new kind of human being. Most hippies in reacting against pressures at home and school, which probably began in kindergarten, are taking what Harvard psychiatrist Eric Ericson has called a "psychological moratorium on life." They have usurped the prerogatives of children to dress up and be irresponsible. . . .

As citizens the hippies are dropping out of a sanctimonious society that condones napalm and racism and imperialism and war, but not marijuana, and whose public officials are insensitive to the problems of the poor, the Negroes and the Vietnamese. As students the hippies are dropping out of a bureaucratic educational system whose teachers are remote and uninterested in them and whose administrators never listen seriously to their complaints. As employees the hippies are dropping out of the vast corporations and unions, which manipulate and depersonalize people rather than liberate them and provide interesting and challenging work. As human beings they are dropping out of a dehumanized American society controlled by a "power elite" that thrives on and perpetuates cold war anticommunism, counter-revolution and American hegemony abroad, and centralized control of economics and politics at home. The American passion, they say, is murder, and all that America really knows is profit and property. . . .

A New Religion?

So extensive has been the hippie impact upon American life that the distinguished Harvard theologian Harvey Cox wrote recently in *Playboy* that "hippieness has all the marks of a new religious movement" and deserves careful attention from theologians. It has its evangelists, its sacred grottoes and its exuberant converts. Haight-Ashbury in San Francisco has become the Holy City of hippiedom welcoming the faithful. Cox writes that the hippies chant Hindu *mantras* in Washington, stroll in threadbare Edwardian finery in Chicago and display vivid face and body paint in Boston. Its adherents prance lovingly in parks and city streets all over the country, petting policemen's horses and pelting squad cars with daffodils. Last Easter Sunday morning they held a love-in in New York's Central Park that was, believes Cox, much closer to the Easter spirit than the parade in front of St. Patrick's Cathedral. "Jesus was here this morning," one beatific pilgrim told an observer, "and so was Buddha."

Nowhere has the hippie movement been more wholeheartedly endorsed than in the religious press. *Christian Century* has published several articles, all either apologetic or eulogistic. In its August 16 issue, for example, historian James Hitchcock reveals that the hippies uphold the religious tradition of the superiority of contemplation to action and preach the "ancient message of Christian asceticism." Hitchcock presents the hippies as a compound of monk, mystic and saint, and credits them with a variety of pietistic and meaningful concerns. . . .

Criticism of Hippie Spirituality

Not all observers, however, are captivated by hippie religiosity. Will Herberg, writing in the *National Review*, proclaims that the hippies are a revival of the Adamites (also known as the Paradisals), a second century small Christian sect that advocated antinomianism, the community of goods, vegetarianism, sexual promiscuity, nudity, emotional self-indulgence, free-floating fantasy thinking and a comprehensive cult of love. Herberg is especially offended by the hippie assumption that man is inherently innocent, a premise that denies original sin. Also theologically offensive is the hippie advocacy of love, which for "them is an orgiastic feeling in which they wallow in self-indulgence," as opposed to the "concern and commitment" that conservative theology would prefer to find at the core of positive effect.

Time magazine ridicules and dismisses the spiritual validity of the hippies' "undigested mixture of drug-induced visions, skimmed Orientalism and nature worship." The hippie religion's outlook is not Judeo-Christian, says *Time*. "Jesus may be revered as the hip *guru* of his time, who preached a primitive form of love power, but Western churches are generally abhorred by the hippies as irrelevant and square.". . .

There are certainly many bizarre and ridiculous features in hippie religion. Arthur Kleps, founder of the largely invisible Neo-American Church, calls his pastors "Boo-Hoos" and employs prayers from Tantric Yoga and Mohawk moccasins in his marriage ceremonies. Timothy Leary, creator of the League for Spiritual Discovery, looks upon the drug LSD as a sacrament whose power to arouse "latent religious sensitivities" forms the wellspring of hippie religiosity: regeneration through chemico-mystical union of the self and the universe, or more commonly, "tuning in." Allen Cohen, editor of the religious journal *Oracle* recommends for religious meditations ouija boards, numerology, Tarot cards, palmistry, Hopi Indian spirits and Henry David Thoreau. While at the Los Angeles–based Oracle Cosmic Joy Fellowship, whose prelates are known as "co-ordinators," worshipers sit cross-legged in an incense-clouded room festooned with Indian print cloths, statues of Buddha and votive candles, holding hands and ecstatically chanting "Om," a Hindu word signifying the ultimate reality.

These absurdities within the hippie religious sects and the propensity of many hippies to voice religious truisms garbed as religious protests have prompted Prof. Hans Toch, who has given us the "Last Word on the Hippies" in *The Nation*, to claim that a great many educated American clerics have become victims of a hippie hang-up. They have converted neutral hippie attributes into virtues, induced the hippies to play religious roles they see prescribed for them, and inadvertently created aberrations that assert that hippies are the vanguard of trends in our society, harbingers of religious and social change who speak for the younger generation. . . .

Perhaps the most astute observer of the impact of hippie religiosity upon the American churches is Dr. Browne Barr, of First Congregational Church, Berkeley, who, writing in the *Christian Century*, depicts the hippies as a new American Gnosticism. Barr is neither a sentimentalist nor an apologist. He believes that the hippies represent a sick and mechanical subculture, that their social manifestations are grossly irresponsible and that their religiosity is a dreadful caricature of the Christian faith. But like other caricatures, especially sincere and honest ones, the new Gnostics of the hippie world speak a word of judgment to the churches: that a religion without ecstasy, without rapture, without a strange warming of the heart, is, as the saying goes, strictly for the birds. . . .

Prophets of the Future?

It is by no means certain that the hippie movement can survive much beyond the summer of 1968. A variety of forces, internal and external, have already appeared to crush it: the hippies' tendency toward anarchy and excesses, the police and the courts, the minority groups and the politicians. Moreover, the hippie world is at bottom a flight from the intellect and all that the intellect implies. It does not really wish to dominate reality; it wishes rather to flee from it. It does not really wish to capture and change the adult world; it wishes to mock it. It possesses many attitudes but no political ideology, and movements without ideology or the discipline necessary for political action have usually ended in disaster.

But though the hippie community may be destined to soon pass from the scene, the roots it feeds upon run deep in our culture. The gap between the young and the old and the contrast between American reality and American ideal both are wide. In this, the hippies' criticism by implication and by action of the "straight" world—its hypocrisy and materialism—may lie their greatest contribution to society.

If the hippies force Americans to look at themselves morally and spiritually naked, they will indeed have accomplished much good. It is entirely possible, however, that they will provoke a blinder and less sensitive reaction. They are playing as dangerously with social passions as any heretic played with religious passions in the Middle Ages. And historians have reminded us countless times how organized society has turned upon those religious heretics, how its inquisitors rooted them out, tortured them, burned them, extirpated their women and children, purged society of their danger.

One cannot now predict the accuracy of the hippie prophets, who compare the impact of their movement with that of early Christianity. The hippie rebellion, it is true, gives some indication of transcending the narrowness of past bohemian revolts, but whether hippies will or can ever compromise with established institutions, as have other successful social movements, cannot be ascertained. Perhaps the hippies by their rejection of compromise are indeed prophets of a future now only dimly perceived.

Women's Liberationists and Radical Feminists

By Irwin Unger and Debi Unger

Early in 1968, groups of radical feminists began meeting to discuss ways to confront society's oppression and objectification of women. According to the writers of this selection, these activists occasionally drew exaggerated conclusions—particularly when they suggested that men and heterosexual relationships were expendable, However, these women's ideas and activism proved to be the harbinger of the latter twentieth-century women's liberation movement. In September 1968 Americans learned about "women's lib" when a group of radical feminists staged a protest at the Miss America Pageant in Atlantic City. In an incident that was later referred to as a "bra-burning," symbols of female objectification—corsets, high heels, and other garments—were tossed into a "freedom ashcan." Irwin Unger and Debi Unger are the authors of *Turning Point: 1968*, a book published in 1988, from which this selection is excerpted.

D uring the early months of 1968, small clusters of women liberationists began to coalesce in cities around the country. In San Francisco the women were New Left dropouts who began to meet for sessions of personal self-examination. Their discussions focused on male oppression and their own sexuality. They came to see, one of their founders reported, that their

Irwin Unger and Debi Unger, *Turning Point: 1968*. New York: Charles Scribner's Sons, 1988. Copyright © 1988 by Irwin Unger and Debi Unger. All rights reserved. Reproduced by permission.

bodies were not their own; they were controlled by "men, doctors, clothes and cosmetic manufacturers, advertisers, churches and schools—everyone but ourselves. . . ." In New Orleans the impetus came from a group of southern white women formerly active in SNCC [Student Nonviolent Coordinating Committee] and the Southern Student Organizing Committee, a Dixie affiliate of SDS [Students for a Democratic Society]. Boston acquired its first Radical Feminist group when Roxanne Dunbar, a West Coast New Leftist, arrived in June and founded Cell 16. Early in 1969 Cell 16 began to publish *No More Fun and Games*, subtitled *A Journal of Female Liberation.*

[Writer Shulamith] Firestone; Pam Allen, a white civil rights activist; Kathie Amatniek, a former . . . peace agitator at Radcliffe College; and Rosalyn Baxandall, the wife of Lee Baxandall, a *Studies on the Left* founder, formed New York Radical Women (NYRW) in the early months of 1968. Shortly after, they were joined by Anne Koedt and Carol Hanisch, two white SNCC workers, Ellen Willis, a pop-music reviewer for *The New Yorker*, and Robin Morgan, a former child actress. Some of these women were Politicos; others Radical Feminists. NYRW mixed activism with introspection. In January [1968] it disrupted the demonstration in Washington of the Jeanette Rankin Brigade, a women's peace group, in order to present its own ceremony celebrating "the burial of traditional womanhood." Amatniek, whose ardent feminism soon induced her to change her name to Kathie Sarachild— to honor her mother rather than her father—delivered a "funeral oration" that defended giving women's issues priority over the Vietnam War. Women's oppression was so closely intertwined with the other injustices in the world, she said, that it could not be postponed until the others were cured. Amatniek's statement was one of the earliest Radical Feminist speeches.

NYRW was also the source of much of the liberationist intellectual arsenal. Its twenty-page mimeographed booklet of June 1968, *Notes From the First Year*, was the first collection of liberationist essays and articles. Many of the pieces were slight, but Ann Koedt's "Myth of the Vaginal Orgasm" would become a classic of liberationist literature and be anthologized a score of times. Later, longer, versions of *Notes* would summarize early liberationist thinking year by year.

NYRW—or at least its Radical Feminist wing—was also the source of consciousness-raising. The practice probably drew from a number of sources. The old Communist left had long used "criticism, self-criticism" sessions to forge a consensus among party members. Mao Tse-tung, Carol Hanisch at one point noted, had used the approach "speak pain to recall pain" to raise political consciousness in Chinese Communist villages. In the South, black congregations had employed "testifying" to express members' religious experiences. Consciousness-raising also resembled group therapy, the precedent probably most familiar to the well-educated women who made up most of the liberationist groups.

Consciousness-raising [CR] started as small Thursday evening gatherings in various New York living rooms where NYRW members could discuss common problems and grievances. Participants were encouraged to express their deepest frustrations and angers. In the early months the consciousness-raising sessions were unstructured and open, with no one managing direction or choosing subjects. This openness soon changed. As prescribed in the "Protective Rules for Consciousness Raising" by Redstockings, a 1969 NYRW offshoot, "sisters" had to reach conclusions that gave the views a political context.

Consciousness-raising was a potent device for making the personal political. But Radical Feminists only considered a part of the personal relevant. Not all grievances were equal. Mothers, sisters, daughters, were exempt from attack; it was primarily the buried grievances of a lifetime against men—fathers, brothers, husbands, lovers, employers—that had political value. Vivien Gornick, a feminist journalist, admitted this bias a few years later. CR sessions, she acknowledged encouraged women to look for explanations of their experiences "in terms of the social and cultural dynamic created by sexism. . . ." They were urged to seek the causes of their personal pain primarily in "the cultural fact of . . . patriarchy." A logical extension of the position was the "prowoman line," which meant, one Redstockings member said, "that we take the woman's side in *everything*."

Exaggerated Grievances

The feminist perceptions of male oppression were surely valid in part. Women *had* been humiliated, degraded, wronged, manipulated, exploited, abused, belittled, and frustrated by men. It could be argued that women over the centuries had done the same things to men, and at times women had been the victims of other women, not just men. But women *had* been the weaker sex, the *second* and lesser sex, through most of history, and it is easy to understand why intelligent, well-educated middle-class American women, living in a time when all hierarchies, all power elites, all establishments were losing their legitimacy, felt they had to get in their licks. With blacks attacking "The Man," it is not so surprising that women should attack men.

Yet it was difficult for most men, and for many traditional women, not to feel that consciousness-raising exaggerated, blew the valid grievances out of proportion. The antimale response at times seemed so unqualified, so total. "We identify the agents of our oppression as men," proclaimed the Redstockings manifesto. "*All men* receive economic, social, and psychological benefits from male supremacy. *All men* have oppressed women." Ti-Grace Atkinson, a firebrand who split with NOW [the National Organization for Women] in the fall of 1968 because it was too moderate and reformist and founded "the Feminists," declared women's oppression by men as "the source of *all* the corrupt values throughout the world." Men had "*robbed* women of their lives." The antimale urge stigmatized the institution of marriage itself. The Feminists early adopted a rule that no more than one-third of its membership could "be participants in either a formal (with legal contract) or informal (i.e., living with a man) instance of an institution of marriage." At times the attack skirted the fanatic. Men were "an obsolete form of life" so destructive to the environment, wrote Cell 16's Betsy Warrior (her party name), that they should be exterminated on ecological grounds. Atkinson claimed that men "constitute a social disease."

The most extreme onslaught of all came from Valerie Solanis. Solanis was an actress with a deep grievance against men who, in June 1968, pushed her way into Andy Warhol's Union Square studio and pumped him full of bullets. Her motives were unusual: Warhol had refused to return one of her movie scripts and insisted on producing it! Angry and confused, Solanis was also verbally bloodthirsty. SCUM, the Society for Cutting Up Men, the organization she founded in 1968, proclaimed that males were limited creatures governed entirely by their sexual needs. A man would do anything to screw—"swim a river of snot, wade nostril-deep through a mile of vomit, if he thinks there'll be a friendly pussy awaiting him." Men were incapable of anything creative. They had made the world "a shitpile." If anything was to get better, women must seize control of the government. This could be accomplished by "fucking up the system, selectively destroying property, and murder." SCUM would "kill all men who are not in the Men's auxiliary of SCUM." The "few remaining" males could continue to "exist out their puny days dropped out on drugs or strutting around in drag . . . or they can go off to the nearest friendly suicide center where they will be quietly, quickly, and painlessly gassed to death."

Solanis was probably a certifiable lunatic, though the courts tried her as sane and sentenced her to three years in jail for the attack on Warhol. But the antimale frenzy cannot be dismissed solely as dementia. Some of it derived from a half-hidden Lesbian agenda pushed by militants.

The Lesbian Agenda

The Lesbian theme first comes to the surface in Anne Koedt's "Myth of the Vaginal Orgasm." In this benchmark essay, Koedt attacked the claim of Freudian psychologists that sexual maturity required that women experience vaginal orgasm. The clitoris, she said, was the actual source of orgasm in women. In effect, the Freudians had accused women of sexual and emotional inadequacy because of a colossal ignorance of the female body. But the essay was far more than a technical argument over anatomy. It had wide implications. As the author of the penis-envy concept to explain female personality, Freud seemed a prime source of modern women's notions of inferiority. Since the vaginal orgasm required penetration, it was easy to see it as another assertion of male supremacy. In effect, for a woman to attain emotional maturity, she must, in Freud's view, depend on a man.

Given his time—the turn of the century—and his place—Hapsburg Vienna—Freud's male-supremacist ideas are not surprising. They were also understandably objectionable to feminists. But there was something else. Do away with the vaginal orgasm and you eliminated the sexual indispensability of men, at least in an anatomical sense. Sex could be a solitary occupation with no qualms. More important, it need not be heterosexual. In fact, since women naturally understood the sexual needs of their own kind better than men, Lesbian sex could be superior to straight sex. As Koedt noted, "Lesbian sexuality could make an excellent case, based on anatomical data, for the extinction of the male organ." This scarcely hidden Lesbian message made the Koedt article famous, or infamous, in early liberationist circles.

If men were not needed for pleasure, there still remained re-production. How could the race continue if heterosexual relations were superseded? At the extreme edge of the women's liberation movement there were minds equal to the challenge. Artifical in-semination or, better still, some sort of parthenogenesis as in frogs, might make males totally extraneous. Firestone, for one, talked not only of abolishing the patriarchal family but also of abolishing the need for the patriarch himself by some sort of "ar-tificial reproduction."

Koedt's 1968 essay was a guarded statement of a Lesbian agenda. Of course, most women liberationists and even most Radical Feminists were straight, but no group within the radical wing of the women's movement had such strong incentive to de-plore the reign of patriarchy as Lesbians, and no group labored as actively to advance Radical Feminist interests. Within the Old Left that same sectarian single-mindedness had always worked to the advantage of the Communist party. Within SDS it had given Progressive Labor the edge over its rivals. Now it helped the Lesbians to impose their sensibility disproportionately on the woman's liberation movement. Ti-Grace Atkinson's Feminists went as far as to insist that heterosexuality reduced women to bondage to men. Marriage was nothing more than "legalized rape" and along with the family "must be destroyed."

Straight feminists sometimes fought back, but they were hand-icapped by the dilemma of an antimale philosophy that made het-erosexual relationships problematical. If you believed men were the oppressors, then why not go all the way and give up on them entirely? It would take years before straight feminists could sort out the contradictions in their attitudes toward men.

Miss America 1968

In early 1968, SDS estimated that there were thirty-five or so small women's liberation groups extant. At this point there could not have been more than a few hundred women actively involved in the radical women's movement, and the general public knew almost nothing of them. In March 1968 *The New York Times*, that gauge of upper-middle-class awareness, carried an article entitled "The Second Feminist Wave" by Martha Lear. It described NOW and its leaders but said nothing of Firestone, Koedt, Amatniek, Dunbar, Morgan, or any of the other liberationists. Then came the September Miss America Pageant in Atlantic City, and women's lib erupted into the American consciousness.

The pageant was a natural target of the liberationists. As they considered the nature of female oppression, they had concluded that the cult of female physical beauty was ultimately a male scheme to keep women distracted, subordinate, and defensive. As a feminist polemic would later phrase it, the ideal women depicted in *Playboy* and in the beauty contests "teach women their role in society, . . . teach them that women are articles of conspicuous consumption in the male market. . . ." It followed that the annual beauty contest ritual in the decaying Jersey Shore resort was a profanation of women, reducing them to pretty things, toys of men. Yet the pageant itself was only one example of enslavement through apparent gallantry. Just as deplorable were the fashions imposed on women, styles that distorted their bodies and hobbled their movements. The three worst offenders were the high-heeled shoe, the corset, and the brassiere.

The two hundred women who descended on Atlantic City in September 1968 to proclaim their disgust were mostly from New York Radical Women. In their call to action, the militants denounced the pageant as a "degrading mindless boob-girlie symbol," "racism with roses," and a "consumer con-game." They intended to conduct a peaceful protest and had negotiated an agreement with Atlantic City Mayor Richard Jackson—concerned over the recent violence at the Democratic presidential convention—to "be orderly and quiet." "We don't want another Chicago," noted one of their leaders, Robin Morgan. The protesters brought with them two key props for their "guerrilla theater": a female puppet with chains dangling from her red, white, and blue bathing suit, and a "freedom ashcan."

Most of the protesters were young, but there were also some gadflies left over from the generation of the 1920s radical Women's Party. One of the oldest was Kathie Amatniek's sixty-five-year-old yellow-hatted grandmother, Martha Berlin, who forgot herself and started to talk to a male reporter until her granddaughter called her back to liberationist rigor.

Barred from the Convention Hall while the audience and judges inside were watching the all-American beauties going through their fatuous paces, the protesters marched up and down the Boardwalk singing a parody version of the pageant theme song, "There She Is, Miss America," in three-part harmony, carrying posters denouncing the sexist performance inside.

Though they would not talk to male reporters, they had no objection whatsoever to being filmed and televised. And they provided great visual copy, ritually shredding a *Playboy* magazine and parading a ram fussily bedecked in yellow and blue ribbons, apparently as a symbolic turnabout. It was all wasted. NBC TV's official version of the Miss America crowning ceremony ignored the protest outside the hall.

The First "Bra-Burning"

The true focus of the ceremonies was the freedom ashcan. Into this receptacle the women tossed a bottle of pink liquid detergent, high-heeled shoes, corsets, eyelash curlers, and at least one bra. Each act of disposal invoked a chant or slogan: "Down with bound feet," for the shoes; "Washing dishes is an atrocity," for the detergent; "No more girdles, no more pain; no more trying to hold the fat in vain," for the corset. There is no record of what the bra chucking called forth. No bra—or anything else, apparently—was ever burned. There had been talk of incinerating the despised objects rather than throwing them out, and at one point Morgan had promised Mayor Jackson that she and her colleagues "wouldn't do anything dangerous, just a symbolic bra-burning." But nothing apparently was incinerated. Yet her remark, the nice alliteration of "bra burner," and the whiff of prewar Nazi book burning, made a spurious brassiere immolation the central ritual in the media account. Radical feminists would protest the "bra burner" label, but the event is inscribed in folk history and will not easily be erased.

The Atlantic City demonstration made the women's liberation movement news. *Life*, the news magazines, and many daily newspapers ran accounts of the event. Much of the coverage was either hostile or derisive. The demonstrators were an ugly bunch of viragos who resented beautiful women out of envy. Or else they were crazies who wanted to deny their womanhood. Who else would burn their bras? The impression the media created may not have been favorable, but it was an impression, and a strong one at that. For the first time the broad public learned that women activists had caught up with blacks and students in the race to challenge mainstream America. The publicity brought new recruits in droves. Morgan later reported that a week before the demonstration no more than 30 women had attended the New York Radical Women's meeting; the week following there were 150.

CHRONOLOGY

January 9: The last unmanned lunar probe, *Surveyor 7*, lands on the moon.

January 30: The Tet Offensive begins in Vietnam.

February 1: Former vice president Richard M. Nixon announces his candidacy for president.

February 8: Former Alabama governor George Wallace declares his third-party presidential candidacy.

February 9: The National Guard seals off the Orangeburg campus of South Carolina State College after three black youths die in a confrontation with police.

February 14: Chicano labor leader Cesar Chavez begins a month-long hunger strike to publicize a grape boycott in support of migrant farmworkers.

February 16: The National Security Council abolishes draft deferments for most graduate students.

February 29: The Kerner Commission report declares that white racism is largely responsible for poverty, frustration, and violence in black neighborhoods.

March 16: New York Democratic senator Robert F. Kennedy announces his candidacy for president. Hundreds of Vietnamese civilians are massacred by the U.S. military in the village of My Lai; the incident is kept secret for a year.

March 31: President Lyndon Johnson announces a cutback in the U.S. bombing campaign in North Vietnam. He also declares his withdrawal from the presidential race.

April 3: Metro-Goldwyn-Mayer releases Stanley Kubrick's film *2001: A Space Odyssey.*

April 4: Civil rights leader Martin Luther King Jr. is assassinated.

April 5–9: Riots break out in major cities in the wake of King's assassination, resulting in at least forty deaths.

April 15: Chicago mayor Richard Daley tells city police to "shoot to kill" arsonists and "shoot to maim" looters in any future rioting.

April 16: In a jury trial, priest and activist Phillip Berrigan is found guilty of impeding draft procedures.

April 17: After receiving criticism, Mayor Daley revises his former instructions and states that rioters "should be restrained if possible by minimum force."

April 23: Black and white student radicals occupy five buildings at Columbia University to protest the university's conservative administrative policies.

April 29: The musical *Hair* opens on Broadway.

April 30: New York City police clear Columbia University of protesters.

May 12: Corretta Scott King officially launches the Poor People's Campaign in Washington, D.C., asking the Johnson administration to approve a "freedom budget" of new federal programs for the impoverished.

May 31: Five hundred demonstrators from the Poor People's Campaign take over an auditorium in the U.S. Department of Health, Education, and Welfare (HEW) and demand to meet with HEW secretary Wilbur Cohen.

June 4: Attorney General Ramsey Clark meets with delegates from the Poor People's Campaign. Robert Kennedy defeats Eugene McCarthy in the California Democratic primary election.

June 5: Kennedy is shot and seriously injured after a campaign speech at a Los Angeles hotel. Jordanian immigrant Sirhan Sirhan is arrested as the gunman.

June 6: Kennedy dies.

June 14: Pediatrician and author Benjamin Spock is convicted of conspiring to encourage draft evasion.

July 7: Johnson signs a bill making flag desecration illegal.

July 24–30: Riots break out in Gary, Indiana, and Cleveland, Ohio.

August 1: Johnson signs a bill providing for large numbers of low-income housing units.

August 5: The Republican National Convention opens in Miami Beach, Florida.

August 8: Nixon wins the Republican Party's presidential nomination and chooses Maryland governor Spiro Agnew as his running mate.

August 19: Tom Wolfe's *The Electric Kool-Aid Acid Test* is published.

August 26: The Democratic National Convention opens in Chicago, Illinois.

August 27: Police use clubs and tear gas to disperse thousands of antiwar protesters at the Chicago convention.

August 28: Vice President Hubert Humphrey receives the Democratic presidential nomination. Violent street battles between police and protesters continue in Chicago, resulting in hundreds of injuries and arrests.

September 8: A California court convicts Black Panther leader Huey Newton of manslaughter for the October 1967 slaying of an Oakland police officer.

November 5: Nixon narrowly defeats Humphrey in the U.S. presidential election.

November 12: The U.S. Supreme Court strikes down a 1928 Arkansas law forbidding the teaching of evolution.

December 13: San Francisco State College is closed because of student protests.

December 21: *Apollo 8* is launched with three astronauts whose mission is to orbit the moon.

December 25: Black high school students in Boston, Massachusetts, riot over demands to form student unions.

FOR FURTHER RESEARCH

The Assassination of Martin Luther King Jr.

Ramsey Clark, "The Need for Police: Don't Shoot the Looter," *Vital Speeches of the Day*, September 1, 1968.

Ed Clayton, *Martin Luther King: The Peaceful Warrior.* Ed. Pat MacDonald. New York: Archway, 1996.

David J. Garrow, *Bearing the Cross: Martin Luther King, Jr., and the Southern Christian Leadership Conference.* New York: William Morrow, 1986.

———, "Pointing Toward a Plot: King's Allies Wonder If His Assassin Really Acted Alone," *Newsweek*, February 17, 1997.

Carolyn Shakespeare, "Black Answer to White Racism," *America*, August 17, 1968.

Time, "The Assassination," April 12, 1968.

The Assassination of Robert F. Kennedy

Pete Hamill, "Why, God, Why?" *Good Housekeeping*, September 1968.

William W. MacDonald, "Robert F. Kennedy," *Christian Century*, July 10, 1968.

Newsweek, "Bobby's Last, Longest Day," June 17, 1968.

Warren Rogers and Stanley Tretick, "The Bob Kennedy We Knew," *Look*, July 9, 1968.

Arthur M. Schlesinger Jr., *Robert Kennedy and His Times.* Boston: Houghton Mifflin, 1978.

Theodore C. Sorensen, "RFK: A Personal Memoir," *Saturday Review*, June 22, 1968.

U.S. News & World Report, "Aftermath of a Tragedy," June 17, 1968.

Black Power

Elaine Brown, *A Taste of Power: A Black Woman's Story.* New York: Doubleday, 1992.

Eldridge Cleaver, *Soul on Ice.* New York: Dell, 1968.

Angela Davis, *Angela Davis: An Autobiography.* New York: Random House, 1974.

Michael Harris, "Black Panthers: The Cornered Cats," *Nation*, July 8, 1968.

George Jackson, *Soledad Brother: The Prison Letters of George Jackson.* New York: Bantam Books, 1970.

Huey Newton, "Huey Newton Speaks from Jail," *motive*, October 1968.

The Chicago Riots

David Farber, *Chicago '68.* Chicago: University of Chicago Press, 1988.

Richard Goldstein, "Theatre of Fear: One on the Aisle," *Village Voice*, September 5, 1968.

Newsweek, "Hippies, Yippies, and Mace," September 2, 1968.

Joseph Roddy, "Father and Son at the Barricades," *Look*, October 15, 1968.

Nora Sayre, "Communal Concussion," *Progressive*, October 1968.

Raymond A. Schroth, "The Other Convention," *America*, September 14, 1968.

Terry Southern, "Grooving in Chi," *Esquire*, November 1968.

Time, "Who Were the Protesters?" September 6, 1968.

Hippies and the Counterculture

Christian Century, "The Free Church of Berkeley's Hippies," April 10, 1968.

Martin Lee and Bruce Shlain, *Acid Dreams: The CIA, LSD, and the Sixties Rebellion.* New York: Grove Press, 1985.

Neal White, "Getting Away from It All Down on the Hog Farm," *New Republic*, February 17, 1968.

Tom Wolfe, *The Electric Kool-Aid Acid Test.* New York: Bantam Books, 1968.

The 1968 Election

Lewis Chester, Godfrey Hodgson, and Bruce Page, *An American Melodrama: The Presidential Campaign of 1968.* New York: Viking, 1969.

David Frost, *The Presidential Debate, 1968.* New York: Stein and Day, 1968.

Lewis L. Gould, *1968: The Election That Changed America.* Chicago: Ivan R. Dee, 1993.

Norman Mailer, "Miami Beach and Chicago," *Harper's Magazine*, November 1968.

Eugene J. McCarthy, *The Year of the People.* Garden City, NY: Doubleday, 1969.

Joe McGinniss, *The Selling of the President, 1968.* New York: Pocket Books, 1970.

Student Protesters and the New Left

Cointelpro. www.cointel.org.

John Gallahue, "White Rage," *America*, October 5, 1968.

Abbie Hoffman, *Soon to Be a Major Motion Picture.* New York: Berkley Books, 1980.

James Simon Kunen, *The Strawberry Statement.* New York: Random House, 1969.

Louis S. Levine, "Why Students Seize Power," *Nation*, May 13, 1968.

Life, "Mutiny at a Great University," May 10, 1968.

Thomas W. O'Brien, "Why Rebels on the Campus?" *America*, October 5, 1968.

Ramparts, "The Siege of Columbia," June 15, 1968.

Arthur M. Schlesinger Jr., "America 1968: The Politics of Violence," *Harper's Magazine*, August 1968.

The Vietnam War

Peter Braestrup, *Big Story: How the American Press and Television Reported and Interpreted the Crisis of Tet 1968 in Vietnam and Washington.* Boulder, CO: Westview Press, 1977.

Tran Van Dinh, "Why the War in Vietnam Cannot Be Won," *Christian Century*, July 24, 1968.

Ronnie E. Ford, *Tet 1968: Understanding the Surprise.* London: Frank Cass, 1995.

Marc Jason Gilbert and William Head, eds., *The Tet Offensive.* Westport, CT: Praeger, 1996.

Tom Lickness, "Vietnam 1968," 1996. www.vietvet.org/vn68.htm.

Robert Shaplen, "Letter from Saigon: Tet Attacks," *New Yorker*, March 23, 1968.

The Women's Liberation Movement

Maron Lockwood Carden, *The New Feminist Movement.* New York: Russell Sage Foundation, 1974.

Sara Evans, *Personal Politics: The Roots of Women's Liberation in the Civil Rights Movement and the New Left.* New York: Vintage, 1980.

Jo Freeman, *The Politics of Women's Liberation.* New York: Longman, 1975.

M.W. Lear, "Second Feminist Wave," *New York Times Magazine*, March 10, 1968.

Gloria Steinem, *Outrageous Acts and Everyday Rebellions.* New York: Holt, Rinehart, and Winston, 1983.

The Year 1968

Carole Fink, Philipp Gassert, and Detlef Junker, *1968: The World Transformed.* New York: Cambridge University Press, 1998.

Charles Kaiser, *1968 in America: Music, Politics, Chaos, Counterculture, and the Shaping of a Generation.* New York: Grove Press, 1988.

Irwin Unger and Debi Unger, *Turning Point: 1968*. New York: Charles Scribner's Sons, 1988.

Jules Witcover, *The Year the Dream Died: Revisiting 1968 in America*. New York: Warner Books, 1997.

Websites

The Digger Archives, www.diggers.org. This is an ongoing Web project to preserve the history of the Diggers, an anarchist guerrilla street theater group that emerged in San Francisco's Haight-Ashbury district during the 1960s. It includes links to articles, chronologies, bibliographies, and a discussion forum.

1968 Revisited, www.nyu.edu/library/bobst/collections/exhibits/ arch/Homepg/Index.html. Created by Amy Surak and presented by the New York University (NYU) Archives, this site offers a historical retrospective of 1968 through the eyes of the NYU student community. It includes a time line, a "who's who" menu, and video clips.

The Psychedelic '60s, www.lib.virginia.edu/speccol/exhibits/ sixties. Compiled by the Special Collections Department at the University of Virginia Library, this site presents a history of the entire decade through a descriptive and detailed catalog of books, art, and music.

Sixties Net, www.sixties.net. This site displays a compilation of historical data, sounds, and images of the 1960s.

Voices from the Underground: Radical Protest and the Underground Press in the "Sixties," www.lib.uconn.edu/~eembardo/ voices/about/htm. This site, compiled by the Thomas J. Dodd Research Center of the University of Connecticut Libraries, offers a descriptive history of the 1960s with links to an archived gallery of images.

The Whole World Was Watching: An Oral History of 1968, www. stg.brown.edu/projects/1968. This site, a project conducted by Brown University's Scholarly Technology Group and several other educational organizations, contains transcripts, audio recordings, interviews, and personal memories about the year 1968. It includes a glossary, a time line, and a bibliography of references.

INDEX